Collins

Edexcel GCSE 9-1
Business

Revision Guide

T0337232

Stephanie Campbell, Helen Kellaway,
Tony Michaelides and Cate Calveley

About this Revision & Practice book

Revise

These pages provide a recap of everything you need to know for each topic.

You should read through all the information before taking the Quick Test at the end. This will test whether you can recall the key facts.

> **Quick Test**
>
> 1. Define the term 'good'.
> 2. Identify **one** purpose of a business.
> 3. List the **three** factors of production that an entrepreneur must organise.

Practise

These topic-based questions appear shortly after the revision pages for each topic and will test whether you have understood the topic. If you get any of the questions wrong, make sure you read the correct answer carefully.

Review

These topic-based questions appear later in the book, allowing you to revisit the topic and test how well you have remembered the information. If you get any of the questions wrong, make sure you read the correct answer carefully.

Mix it Up

These pages feature a mix of questions for the different topics within a chapter. They will make sure you can recall the relevant information to answer a question without being told which topic it relates to.

Test Yourself on the Go

Visit our website at **collins.co.uk/collinsGCSErevision** and print off a set of flashcards. These pocket-sized cards feature questions and answers so that you can test yourself on all the key facts anytime and anywhere. You will also find lots more information about the advantages of spaced practice and how to plan for it.

Workbook

This section features even more topic-based questions as well as practice exam papers, providing further practice opportunities for each topic to guarantee the best results.

ebook

To access the ebook revision guide visit **collins.co.uk/ebooks** and follow the step-by-step instructions.

QR Codes

Found throughout the book, the QR codes can be scanned on your smartphone for extra practice and explanations.

A QR code in the Revise section links to a Quick Recall Quiz on that topic. A QR code in the Workbook section links to a video working through the solution to one of questions on that topic.

Contents

Contents

Quick Recall Quiz

The Dynamic Nature of Business

You must be able to:

- Discuss the different reasons why new business ideas emerge
- Discuss how new business ideas emerge.

Starting a Business

- Businesses produce goods and services to meet customer needs.
- Businesses are referred to as **dynamic**; the **goods** they produce and **services** they offer must continuously change in line with the changing tastes of customers and the market.
- A business that stays up to date will have a better chance of growth and survival.
- There are three main reasons that new business ideas are created:
  - changes in technology
  - changes in **consumers**' tastes
  - products and services becoming obsolete.

Changes in Technology

- The evolution of today's Internet and developments in smart technology have led to new business opportunities.
- Smart technology and apps have given rise to the introduction of new accessories that consumers can control from their phones, e.g. smart home devices, fitness devices and health-tracking watches.
- Robotics have paved the way for unassisted vacuum cleaning and mopping.
- Digital services have created new markets for customisation, photo editing and printing.
- Technology supported by artificial intelligence (AI), sensors and other complex software has created new product ideas for car manufacturers, such as driverless cars.

Changes in Consumers' Tastes

- Changes in consumers' tastes can increase the popularity of particular goods and services.
- Changes in consumers' dietary requirements have created a bigger market for plant-based foods and non-diary milk products, and businesses respond by making more of these products.
- The rise in dessert culture has led to the opening of new dessert parlours on the high street.

> **Key Point**
>
> Business ideas are created owing to changes in technology, changes in consumer tastes, or products and services becoming obsolete.

> **Key Point**
>
> The rise in the use of technology has created many new business ideas.

- Consumers have become more health conscious, giving rise to new gym chains, the need for personal trainers, and fitness-related goods and services.
- As consumers become more environmentally aware, they favour organic, free range products and goods that use recyclable packaging.

Obsolete Goods and Services

- As products become outdated, they are replaced with new business ideas that better meet the needs of consumers.
- USBs have become outdated and have been replaced with the use of cloud storage, which removes the risk of losing or damaging important files.
- More consumers are opting to buy electric cars rather than petrol cars as they are less damaging to the environment.
- Alarm clocks and digital cameras have become outdated as consumers prefer to use smartphones.

Cloud Storage

How is a New Business Idea Generated?

- A new business idea will either be generated to fill a **gap in the market** or to improve an existing business idea.
- An **entrepreneur** may have an original idea (e.g. a virtual keep-fit device) or they may develop an existing business idea to make it more efficient or better meet the needs of customers (e.g. creating a grocery delivery service in an area).
- A business idea may even come about by accident.

Key Point

A new business idea will either be original or will be a better version of an existing good/service.

Key Words

dynamic business
goods
services
consumers
gap in the market
entrepreneur

Quick Test

1. Explain how dynamic businesses can respond to customer wants.
2. Give **three** reasons why new business ideas come about.
3. Define the term 'obsolete'.

Risk and Reward

Quick Recall Quiz

You must be able to:

- Understand that entrepreneurs must establish potential risks and plan for them when starting up a new business
- Explain the potential rewards for starting up a new business.

Risk

- It is important for an entrepreneur to understand the things that can go wrong when setting up a new business; these are **risks**.
- Risk occurs at every stage in business. However, the early stages present the most risks for entrepreneurs as customers are not familiar with the business and there may be strong, established competition in the market.
- If an entrepreneur can address the risks during the development stage of a new business idea, they can be mitigated (reduced) and there is more chance of success.
- Risks include: business failure, financial loss, lack of security.
- Business failure can be caused by:
  - entrepreneurs not knowing their market well
  - not having enough money to start a business
  - poor decision making
  - competition or goods/services not meeting the needs of customers.

- An entrepreneur can lose the money they have put into the business and any money borrowed from other sources.
- Many small businesses operate as sole traders and partnerships, as these have unlimited liability; these are the riskiest business start-up options (see pages 38–39).
- Business owners can also lose personal possessions if the business runs up debts.

> **Key Point**
>
>
>
> Risks can include business failure, loss of money and lack of a secure income.

> **Key Point**
>
>
>
> Although risks can cause businesses to fail, with careful planning and research the risks can be reduced.

- Working for yourself means you do not have the security of a regular salary or wages. If a business is not successful, an entrepreneur can be at risk of not being able to pay bills such as rent or a mortgage.
- It is important for entrepreneurs to plan for potential risks and conduct relevant market research to understand how their product will/will not meet customer needs.

Reward

- The **rewards** for starting up a new business can include: business success, profit and personal independence.
- Some rewards are connected to money and are referred to as 'financial rewards'; other rewards are non-financial, e.g. independence.
- Measuring the sales of the business, the amount of market share it holds or the profit made over time are ways of determining commercial success.
- Success can mean different things to different entrepreneurs, e.g. an online fashion blogger may consider subscribers or followers as a way of determining success, whereas a personal trainer will consider getting his/her clients to their desired weight/level of fitness as success.

- **Profit** is the difference between the revenue earned by a business and the costs of a business. Any profit that is gained goes to the business owner(s).
- An entrepreneur will make all the decisions for the business and can set what days they want to work. This independence is rewarding and encourages people to start their own businesses.

Key Point

Having a successful business, making a profit or being independent are potential rewards for starting up a business.

Key Point

Business revenue, costs and profit are covered on pages 28–29.

Key Words

risks
rewards
profit

Quick Test

1. Identify **three** risks a start-up business may face.
2. Identify ways in which entrepreneurs can reduce the risk of business failure.
3. Identify the non-financial rewards a business start-up can provide.

The Role of Business Enterprise

Quick Recall Quiz

You must be able to:

- Understand that the purpose of businesses is to produce goods and services, meet consumers' needs and add value
- Outline the different ways a business can add value to its products to increase worth
- Explain that the role of an entrepreneur is to organise resources, make business decisions and take risks.

Purposes of Businesses

Produce Goods and Services

- A business will either provide **goods** or **services** to consumers.
- A good is a physical product that can be touched, e.g. a pair of trainers or a mobile phone.
- Services are non-physical, e.g. a driving lesson or a taxi ride.
- **Product** is a generic term used for both goods and services.

Meet Customer Needs

- Providing what consumers want is at the heart of a successful start-up.
- A business owner needs to ensure their goods or services satisfy the needs of their consumers for the business to be successful.
- If consumers' needs are not met, they may not wish to buy the goods or services and the business will be at risk of failure.
- Often there are different businesses producing similar products, giving consumers a choice to buy from whoever most meets their needs.

Add Value

- An important purpose of a business is to add value to its goods/services.
- Adding value is the difference between the cost of inputs (e.g. raw materials/components) and the price that consumers are willing to pay for them.
- Supermarkets add value to fruit. Fruit that is chopped is more expensive as it has been through a process to make it easier to eat than whole fruit.
- Methods to add value include:
  - branding
  - quality
  - design
  - convenience
  - unique selling points (USPs).

> **Key Point**
>
> Goods are physical products. Services are non-physical.

> **Key Point**
>
> Consumer needs are covered on pages 14–15.

> **Key Point**
>
> Methods of adding value include: branding, quality, convenience, design and unique selling points.

- **Branding** – this creates an image for a product that sets it apart from competitors and makes it easily recognisable by consumers; consumers will pay a higher price for a branded product (e.g. a designer fashion label) than an unbranded product.
- **Quality** – if a business provides a high-quality product, consumers will be prepared to pay a higher price, as they know it is premium, e.g. a restaurant that uses the best cuts of meat.
- **Design** – if a product has a unique feature or design, this makes it different from other products; consumers are willing to pay a higher price for something that has a special design or feature, e.g. a handmade product.
- **Convenience** – consumers are willing to pay more for a product if it saves them time, e.g. pre-chopped vegetables.
- **USPs** – this is a characteristic or feature of a product that makes the product unique, and makes it harder for another business to copy, e.g. a special cake recipe.

- A successful business will likely use more than one method to add value.
- If a business can add value and keep costs low, the amount of profit will be increased.

The Role of an Entrepreneur

- An entrepreneur's role is to organise resources needed to produce goods and services, make decisions to best manage the resources and to take risks that will lead to success for the business.
- To provide goods and services in business, an entrepreneur will need four things: capital, land, labour and enterprise. These are known as the four **factors of production**:
  - **capital**: human-made resources (goods used to produce other goods)
  - **land**: all natural resources, e.g. wheat or solar power
  - **labour**: human input, e.g. skills or qualifications
  - **enterprise**: skills and characteristics to manage the other three factors (capital, land, labour) and take risks.
- It is an entrepreneur's responsibility to organise the four factors of production to make goods and services that consumers want to buy.
- Organising these factors is risky and an entrepreneur must take careful consideration before making decisions.

Key Point
The four factors of production are: capital, land, labour and enterprise.

 Quick Test

1. Define the term 'good'.
2. Give **one** purpose of a business.
3. List the **three** factors of production that an entrepreneur must organise.

Key Words
product
add value
unique selling points
factors of production
enterprise

1 Explain **one** reason why a business needs to be dynamic. [3]

_____

_____

_____

_____

2 Give **one** benefit from taking advantage of a gap in the market. [1]

_____

3 Which **one** of the following is **not** an example of why new business ideas come about?
Select **one** answer. [1]

A Changes in technology ☐ **C** Businesses are not innovative ☐

B Changes in what consumers want ☐ **D** Goods/services becoming obsolete ☐

4 Give **one** way in which changing customer preferences impact businesses. [1]

_____

5 Define the term 'risk'. [1]

_____

6 Explain **one** reason why independence is a reward for starting up a business. [3]

_____

_____

_____

_____

7 Explain **one** reason how a lack of security is seen as a risk for an entrepreneur. [3]

_____

_____

_____

_____

8 Which **one** of the following would **not** contribute to business failure?
Select **one** answer.   [1]

A Not meeting the needs of
   customers ☐   C Having a business plan ☐

                                  D Not having the finance to cover
B Poor decision making ☐   all start-up costs ☐

9 Give **two** purposes of a business.   [2]

_____

_____

10 Explain **one** reason why enterprise is an important factor of production. [3]

_____

_____

_____

_____

11 Give **five** ways in which a business can add value to its goods or services. [5]

_____

_____

_____

_____

_____

12 Explain how branding adds value to a business's products.   [3]

_____

_____

_____

_____

Customer Needs

Quick Recall Quiz

You must be able to:

- Identify and understand the different customer needs
- Explain the importance of businesses adapting to accommodate customer needs
- Evaluate possible rewards for businesses that meet their customers' needs.

What are Customer Needs?

- **Customer needs** are the specific wants or needs buyers have when purchasing a product.
- Customer needs include:
  - price
  - quality
  - choice
  - convenience.
- To spot opportunities in the market, an entrepreneur must understand what customers desire and aim to meet their needs with the business idea.

> **Key Point**
>
> The four key customer needs are price, quality, choice and convenience.

How do Businesses Meet Customer Needs?

- Customers don't all want the same things from a business. Think about it, do you watch the same films as your grandparents? Different businesses exist to provide choice to customers.
- Businesses produce goods and services that will satisfy the different wants of customers. For example, Netflix has a variety of films available; subscribers can choose between different age ranges to suit them, and different movie styles, depending on what they want to watch.
- Meeting the needs of the customer often requires a combination of having a suitable price that they will pay for a product and quality that meets their expectations.
- Products can have different features to provide choice to a customer, e.g. different colour options for trainers.

> **Key Point**
>
> Businesses keep in touch with their customers through market research (see pages 16–17).

- The product also has to be made available so it is convenient to buy when the customer needs it.
- As time passes, trends lose and gain in popularity and so customers will want different things from what they buy. To stay successful, a business needs to keep up to date with what is in demand. Businesses need regular contact with their customers (e.g. through social media) to keep up to date.

Why is it Important for Businesses to Adapt to Meet Customer Needs?

- It's important for businesses to adapt so that:
  - they can target lots of different customers
  - the same product can satisfy different customer needs
  - a business does not lose customers to competitors
  - the business can stay current and on trend.

How are Price and Quality Linked?

- Customers will try to get the best quality for the most reasonable price, e.g. a customer may be willing to pay more for a burger from one business than another because they believe it uses better ingredients.
- Businesses need to ensure they price their goods or services at the right level, according to the quality that customers expect.

Why Meeting Customer Needs is Important

- Businesses can only survive if they have customers – so they have to focus on what their customers want.
- A business must have enough customers willing to pay a high enough price to cover costs and make a profit.
- Satisfied customers lead to more sales and revenue for a business.
- Other rewards of satisfied customers include: profit, good **customer reviews**, word of mouth, **repeat purchases**, loyal customers.

> ### Key Point
>
> Businesses need to achieve the right balance to meet customer needs, e.g. a company may have a good choice of products but if they are priced too high they will not meet the needs of customers who want or need low prices.

> ### Quick Test
>
> 1. Give **three** different customer needs.
> 2. Give **one** reason why a business would want to provide choice to customers.
> 3. Give **one** reason why a customer might pay more for a flight on British Airways than they would for an easyJet flight.
> 4. Explain **one** reason why meeting customer needs is so important to a business.

> ### Key Words
>
> customer needs
> customer reviews
> repeat purchases

Market Research

Quick Recall Quiz

You must be able to:

- Define and explain the purpose of market research
- Give examples of how businesses collect market research data
- Discuss how a business uses data collected from market research.

What is Market Research?

- **Market research** is the process of collecting information about what consumers want, **market trends** and competitors.
- For a small start-up business, market research will be focused on finding out if there is enough demand to make the business idea successful. The business may not have large enough budgets to carry out widespread research.
- Market research helps entrepreneurs identify and understand customer needs.
- It can be used to:
  - identify a gap in the market
  - inform business decisions
  - reduce the risk of starting a business.

Primary Research

- **Primary research** is collecting new information that meets the specific needs of a business.
- The information will not have been collected before.
- Examples include: survey, questionnaire, focus group, observation.

Advantages
• Can ask questions that they need answers to
• The information is current
• The information won't have been seen by competitors

Disadvantages
• Can be expensive
• Can be time-consuming
• The results may be inaccurate

Secondary Research

- **Secondary research** involves using data that already exists, or data that has already been gathered by someone else.
- Examples include: Internet, market reports, government reports.

Advantages
• The data is easy to find
• Cheap or free to obtain
• Can give a good overview of the market

Disadvantages
• It may have been collected for a different purpose and so may be inaccurate
• Can be out of date
• May not be specific to the business needs

> **Key Point**
>
> Business decisions should be based on information collected from market research.

> **Key Point**
>
> Small start-up businesses are not likely to have a large sum of money for market research. This will limit the methods they can use.

Social Media and Market Research Data

- **Social media** can be used by entrepreneurs to collect research via feedback from comments, reviews, surveys or online focus groups about their business or to find out how customers feel about competitors.
- Current trends can be tracked using hashtags and by following popular posts.
- The greater the activity on social media, the more likely it is that a business will receive responses to market research.
- Collecting data can be quick and cheap.
- The data can be collected in real time so is up to date.
- Businesses can respond to their customers immediately.
- The data collected can be used to inform business decisions.

Qualitative and Quantitative Data

- **Quantitative data** is numerical and can be measured easily.
- Closed questions from a questionnaire can be put into a graph or chart.
- **Qualitative data** is opinions, judgements and feelings, and so cannot be put into a numerical form.
- Qualitative data can be collected during focus groups, in which open-ended questions are asked to gain in-depth answers.
- Quantitative and qualitative data should be used together to inform decision making.
- Qualitative and quantitative data can be derived from both primary and secondary market research.

Considering Data Before Use

- A business must determine how reliable research is before making decisions based upon it.
- Market research can be misleading if the right information is not collected from the right people.
- Market research may be unreliable as questions can be worded in a way that lead people to a certain answer, respondents may not give true answers, and the sample of people used for the research may not be large enough to determine how the entire market feels.
- Businesses can be successful without conducting any market research, e.g. innovation can come from designing a product first.
- Research data needs to be regularly reviewed in line with changing business decisions.
- Businesses should use a combination of different research methods and data to inform decisions.

Quick Test

1. Define the term 'market research'.
2. Give **two** types of market research.
3. Give the name for the type of data that can be interpreted in a numerical way.

Market Segmentation

You must be able to:

- Explain how businesses identify and use market segmentation to target customers
- Discuss how market mapping can identify gaps in the market and the competition.

What is Market Segmentation?

- **Market segmentation** involves breaking down a market into smaller groups, called segments.
- Each of the different groups will contain people that have similar characteristics and have similar wants and needs.
- Information from market research will usually determine which market segment to target goods or services at.
- A business can then focus on how best to sell to that **target market** and meet the customer needs of that group.

How are Markets Segmented?

By Location
- Grouping customers based on where they live.
- A business may decide to focus on selling to customers in a small local area, e.g. a café, or in a busy town.

By Demographics
- Grouping customers based on statistical data relating to the population (**demographics**), e.g. resident status – home owner or renter.
- A business may consider whether it is targeting families or couples for its product.

By Lifestyle
- Grouping customers on how they live their lives and the choices they make.
- With more consumers becoming concerned about climate change, businesses are placing greater importance on reusable and recyclable packaging.

By Income
- Grouping customers based on how much they earn, the job that they do or their social class.
- If a business has a luxury good or service, it will target customers with high earnings.

By Age
- Grouping customers according to their age.
- An app developer may make learning apps aimed at teaching the alphabet to toddlers or times tables to primary school-aged children.

> **Key Point**
>
> Markets can be segmented by location, demographics, lifestyle, income and age.

Market Mapping

- When a business has decided on a market segment to target, it needs to decide what is important to that market and where to place its product within this market.
- A diagram can be used to position and compare products in a market; this diagram is called a **market map**.
- Market mapping is used by businesses to identify where a product will be placed in a market compared to other similar products in the same market.
- A diagram is drawn up with two axes and each axis represents a feature of the market. These features are based on the needs of the target market.
  These features can be:
  - high price – low price
  - high quality – low quality
  - large range of services – small range of services
  - very colourful – no colour.
- Goods or services from different businesses are placed on the map according to how they meet the features.
- Products can be differentiated based on the features to make a business's product stand out.
- A business can look for gaps in the market map to identify possible business opportunities.
- Competitors can be identified and businesses can look for ways to improve on what they are offering.
- A business must take caution when identifying gaps in the market. The gap may be due to there being no market available. For example, customers will not buy a product that has a high price but is of low quality.

Example of a market map

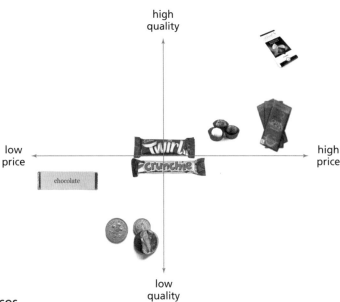

> ### Key Point
>
> Market mapping is key to finding out gaps in the market and the identity of competitors.

Quick Test

1. Define the term 'market segmentation'.
2. Give **four** ways a market can be segmented.
3. Define the term 'market map'.
4. Give **one** benefit to a business owner of using a market map.

Key Words

market segmentation
target market
demographics
market map

The Competitive Environment

You must be able to:

- Understand that businesses operate in a competitive environment
- Discuss the strengths and weaknesses of competitors
- Discuss the impact of competition on business decision making.

Competitive Environment

- Small start-up businesses must be aware of, and investigate, other businesses offering similar goods/services.
- Competition occurs when separate businesses provide goods and services to the same group of customers.
- A **competitive environment** is a market where there are many businesses selling similar goods and services, e.g. consider the choice available when buying a smartphone – this is a competitive environment.
- Businesses operating in competitive environments need to find ways to make their goods and services different from the competition; this is referred to as **differentiation**.
- To investigate the strengths and weaknesses of potential competition, a business will look at different criteria.

Do you know what your Competitors are doing?

How do Businesses Compete?

Price

- One business may offer lower prices to attract consumers.
- Price lowering can result in more sales but will also increase costs for the business, as it must produce more to meet the increased demand; if the business doesn't make enough extra sales, its overall revenue may be less than before and thus profits may be lower.
- Reducing prices may also encourage other businesses to reduce prices as well, creating a price war. If prices are reduced too much, consumers associate the goods or services with poor quality.

Quality

- A business may decide to focus on quality and choose to offer better quality goods/services.
- A high-quality product can attract consumers who want a good quality product, and are also willing to pay a higher price.
- Using better quality raw materials or ingredients, or offering additional customer support, will increase costs for a business.

> **Key Point**
>
> Businesses need to consider the strengths and weaknesses of competitors based on: price, quality, location, product range and customer service.

Location

- A business may have a superior location over another business – it may be easy to access and be more convenient for consumers – resulting in higher sales.
- A factory may have good transport links for suppliers and distribution.
- An online business may have a more user-friendly website.
- A business may not be able to change location but can instead focus on offering more to customers, e.g. free Wi-Fi or comfortable seating.

Product Range

- Having a large **product range** gives consumers more choice and businesses can meet different customer needs.
- A business may decide to specialise in a specific good or service and this will attract consumers who want a more dedicated service.

Customer Service

- A business can decide to compete through offering a good selling experience or excellent after-sales service.
- Good customer service can help to secure repeat custom.
- Satisfied consumers leave good reviews and provide word-of-mouth recommendations.
- Training staff in good customer service can increase training costs.

Competition and Decision Making

- Operating in a competitive environment is more challenging for a small start-up business. Rather than trying to match the strengths of competitors, a small business will need to focus on differentiating its goods/services.
- Market research is crucial to stay up to date with the actions of competitors.
- Once a business can identify potential opportunities to better meet customer needs, it can improve what it has on offer.
- A business can gain a **competitive advantage** by:
    - buying cheaper raw materials to make cost savings
    - offering exceptional customer service
    - providing excellent quality
    - offering promotions and loyalty discounts.

Key Words

competitive environment
differentiation
product range
competitive advantage

1 Which **one** of the following is an example of a product becoming outdated?
Select **one** answer. [1]

A Portable CD players ☐

B Smartphones ☐

C Virtual reality headsets ☐

D Cloud storage ☐

2 Discuss the benefit to a business of changes in technology. [6]

_____

_____

_____

_____

_____

_____

_____

_____

3 Explain **one** way in which business can adapt an existing commercial idea. [3]

_____

_____

_____

_____

_____

4 Which **two** of the following are potential rewards for setting up a business?
Select **two** answers. [2]

A Owning a successful business ☐

B Cash-flow forecast ☐

C Making a profit ☐

D Productivity ☐

E Longer working hours ☐

5 Which **one** of the following is an example of a risk for a sole trader?
Select **one** answer. [1]

A Independence ☐

B Sharing financial decisions ☐

C Market research ☐

D Unlimited liability ☐

6 Explain **one** way an entrepreneur can avoid risks when starting up a new business. [3]

7 Explain **one** reason why a business adds value to its goods and services. [3]

8 Explain **one** way in which design helps a business to add value. [3]

1 Define the term 'customer needs'. [1]

2 Give **one** reason why customer needs differ. [1]

3 Explain **one** reason why it is important for a business to identify customer needs. [3]

4 Which **two** of the following are examples of primary market research?
Select **two** answers. [2]

A Questionnaire ☐

B Market reports ☐

C The Internet ☐

D Newspapers ☐

E Observation ☐

5 Identify **one** factor that limits the market research methods of start-up businesses. [1]

6 Explain **one** way in which businesses can use social media to collect market research data. [3]

7 Define the term 'quantitative data'. [1]

....

....

8 Which **two** of the following are examples of how markets can be segmented?
Select **two** answers. [2]

A Aesthetics ☐

B Productivity ☐

C Demographics ☐

D Age ☐

E Transport ☐

9 Discuss the impact of competition on a business's decision making. [6]

....

....

....

....

....

....

....

....

....

Business Aims and Objectives

Quick Recall Quiz

You must be able to:

- Explain what business aims and objectives are when starting up
- Understand the difference between financial and non-financial aims and objectives
- Analyse why aims and objectives differ between businesses.

What are Aims and Objectives?

- **Aims** are long-term goals for a business; they explain what a business wants to achieve in the future.
- **Objectives** are the short-term steps a business takes to achieve its aims.
- **SMART** objective setting is often used to make sure objectives are specific, measurable, achievable, realistic and timely.

> **Key Point**
>
> Aims and objectives can vary for different types of organisations and can be financial or non-financial.

Why Does a Business Set Aims and Objectives?

- To allow the business to share its direction with staff so they know what to focus on and are motivated to perform.
- To enable a business to measure its performance.
- To help a business plan for the future.

Financial Aims and Objectives for Different Types of Organisations

- Private sector businesses often have aims and objectives that maximise their **profit**, **market share** or business growth.
- Private sector businesses are privately owned.
- Public sector businesses are more likely to focus on delivering a service to customers and keeping costs to a minimum.
- Public sector businesses are run by the government for the benefit of society, e.g. schools, hospitals and fire services.
- Not-for-profit organisations, or charities, aim to fundraise or collect donations for specific causes, e.g. The Royal Society for the Prevention of Cruelty to Animals (RSPCA).
- Social enterprises use business techniques to sell products or services for profit, which is invested to benefit society or the environment, rather than paid out to individual shareholders, e.g. Divine Chocolate.

Financial Aims and Objectives

- Financial aims and objectives typically relate to money.
- When a business starts trading, often its aim is **survival**, which means to be able to simply operate (survive) by meeting its costs in the beginning stages, which tend to be high.
- Many businesses aim to maximise profit.
- Some businesses aim to increase the volume of **sales** of goods or services.
- Other businesses have an aim to increase their market share, which is the percentage of sales held by a business in a particular market.
- Some entrepreneurs begin a business to provide them with **financial security** and personal wealth.

Non-financial Aims and Objectives

- Non-financial aims and objectives relate to goals which are not money-related.
- Having a business with **social objectives** (e.g. providing goods and services that are environmentally sustainable or aim to eliminate poverty) is important for many organisations.
- **Personal satisfaction** is a key non-monetary objective, being able to overcome the challenges of running a business successfully.
- Many entrepreneurs aim to challenge themselves with new ventures.
- Some entrepreneurs aim for independence so that they don't have to work for someone else.
- Having more control over their work/life balance might be an aim for some entrepreneurs.

Key Point

A social enterprise is an organisation that raises **capital** for good causes by using traditional business techniques. All profits are reinvested back into the cause, rather than shared out to shareholders.

Key Words

aims
objectives
SMART
profit
market share
survival
sales
capital
financial security
social objectives
personal satisfaction

Quick Test

1. Define the term 'objective'.
2. Explain **one** reason why a business should set aims and objectives.
3. a) Give **one** example of a 'financial' aim.
   b) Give **one** example of a 'non-financial' aim.

Revise

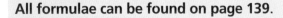

Business Revenues, Costs and Profit

You must be able to:

- Understand the concept and know how to calculate different business formulae relating to revenues, costs and profit
- Calculate total interest as a percentage of total repayment for a mortgage or loan
- Identify break-even levels of output and margins of safety on break-even diagrams, and interpret impacts of change in revenues and costs.

All formulae can be found on page 139.

Revenues, Costs and Profit

Most businesses will face **one-off costs** when they first begin to pay for machinery and property, and will make an initial **loss** because it takes time to attract paying customers.

	Revenue	Fixed costs	Variable costs	Total costs	Profit (loss)
Definition	Cash inflows	Cash outflows that stay the same regardless of the **level of output**	Cash outflows that vary with the level of output	All costs added together are **total costs**	The amount of **revenue** left after deduction of costs; a positive figure is profit, a negative figure is a loss
Formula	selling price × units sold	total costs – **variable costs**	variable cost per unit × number of units sold	**fixed costs +** variable costs	revenue – total costs
Example/s	Revenue for the sale of goods or services	Salaries, rent, advertising	Wages, raw materials, packaging	n/a	n/a

Interest

- Sometimes a business needs to raise finance by borrowing money.
- This borrowing can come from friends or family who are willing to help, or from a bank.
- The business will probably have to pay an **interest rate** on the money borrowed.
- Interest rates charged are expressed as a percentage per annum (p.a.), e.g. 2% p.a. So, for example, if a business borrows £10 000 from a bank for one year at 2% p.a., it will need to repay the bank £10 200 at the end of the year.
- A business may make enough profit to put some cash into a savings account with a bank which pays interest – this is often a way for a business to earn extra revenue as the interest it receives on its savings provides more income.
- Interest is covered in more detail on pages 32–33.

Contribution, Break Even and Margin of Safety

- A business can use formulae for **contribution per unit**, **break even** and **margin of safety** to determine the impact of selling prices and the costs of making and selling products.

	Contribution per unit	Break even	Margin of safety
Definition	How much each sale contributes towards fixed costs; any further sales are a contribution towards profit	Where total costs = total revenue; at this point, a business is not making any loss or any profit	The amount of products made and sold beyond the break-even point up to the actual level of output
Formula	selling price – variable costs per unit	fixed costs ÷ contribution per unit	total output – break-even point

Worked Example

- Cookies are sold at a price of £1
- Fixed costs of £10 000 per month
- Variable costs of 20p per cookie
- 15 000 cookies are made and sold each month

- Therefore:
  - Contribution is £1 – 20p = 80p per cookie
  - Break even is £10 000 ÷ 80p = 12 500 cookies
  - Margin of safety is 15 000 – 12 500 cookies = 2500 cookies

Key Point

Beware, break even relies on products being made and sold. If a business makes no sales, it will not break even.

Break Even

- Using a break-even chart (or diagram) is a visual way of showing where total revenue meets total costs; the break-even point is where the total revenue line crosses the total costs line.
- Break even is a useful tool for a business to calculate how many products or services it needs to make and sell at a certain selling price in order to cover all of its costs.
- Any change in selling price or total costs will have an affect on the break-even point, e.g. if the selling price increases, fewer products will need to be sold.

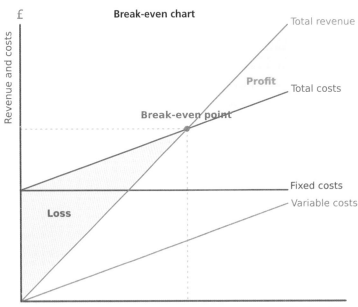

Break-even chart

Quick Test

1. Define 'fixed costs' and 'variable costs'.
2. List **two** examples of 'fixed costs' and **two** examples of 'variable costs'.
3. Define the term 'contribution per unit'.

Key Words

one-off costs
loss
level of output
total costs
revenue
variable costs

fixed costs
interest rate
contribution per unit
break even
margin of safety

Quick Recall Quiz

Cash and Cash-flow

You must be able to:

- Explain the importance of cash to a business
- Understand the difference between cash and profit
- Calculate and interpret cash-flow forecasts.

What is Cash-flow?

- **Cash-flow** is the flow of cash in and out of a business.
- **Cash inflow** is cash paid into a business from a variety of sources, e.g. sales, payments from customers, bank interest, sale of assets, bank loan capital.
- **Cash outflow** is cash paid out of a business, e.g. suppliers, wages, loan repayments, overheads, advertising costs.
- A cash surplus (also known as positive net cash-flow) is when a business experiences more cash inflows than cash outflows over the same period.
- A cash deficit is when a business experiences more cash outflows than cash inflows over the same period (also known as a negative cash-flow).

> **Key Point**
>
> Net cash-flow is the difference between cash inflows and cash outflows.

Why is Cash-flow so Important?

- Cash is critical to the survival of a business.
- Having too little cash when bills are due is known as **insolvency**, which means the business will fail if it cannot pay its bills on time.
- Having too much cash means the business is earning minimal returns in interest, so it would be better to invest the money in new machinery to increase production or put it into a savings account that pays interest.

> **Key Point**
>
> If a business is unable to pay its bills, it risks becoming insolvent, which means being unable to pay debts when they are due.

The Difference Between Cash and Profit

- **Cash** is the money available to the business that can be used to pay for expenses such as wages and raw materials.
- **Profit** is: total revenue – total costs and is calculated immediately after a sale.
- A business may be highly profitable but if it does not have sufficient cash to pay its bills when they are due it risks becoming insolvent, leading to business failure.

> **Key Point**
>
> Profit and cash aren't the same thing. Profit is recorded immediately after a sale, whereas cash is recorded as and when it is received into or spent by a business.

What is a Cash-flow Forecast?

- Cash inflows and outflows are rarely the same amount each month so cash levels in a business fluctuate.
- **Cash-flow forecasts** show future cash inflows and outflows and are normally shown on a weekly or monthly basis.
- The **opening balance** for each month is the same amount as the **closing balance** from the previous month.

How a cash-flow forecast can help a business	
Predicts when cash flows in and out of a business	Financially plan ahead to minimise unexpected cash fluctuations
Highlights future cash surpluses and deficits	Make comparisons with previous periods to identify cash improvements or deterioration
Can be referred back to after cash transactions have been made to check they were correctly forecast	Be more financially accurate, which can help with overall business planning

What can Affect a Cash-flow Forecast?

- Sales might not be consistent.
- Customers might be unable to pay, meaning cash inflows will be less than forecast.
- Costs may change or unexpected costs may occur.
- Ordering too much stock.

Ways to Improve Cash-flow

A business can improve cash-flow by:
- Encouraging customers to pay up front.
- Sending prompt invoices.
- Chasing late payments from customers.
- Selling debts to a factoring company.
- Selling assets.
- Negotiating supplier trade credit terms.
- Using just in time stock ordering methods (see page 92).
- Arranging an overdraft facility to allow for negative balances.

(see page 92)

cash-flow
cash inflow
cash outflow
insolvency
cash-flow forecast
opening balance
closing balance

> ### Quick Test
>
> 1. Define the term 'cash-flow forecast'.
> 2. Give **one** reason why cash-flow is so important to a business.
> 3. Give **three** ways in which a business can improve its cash-flow.

Sources of Business Finance

You must be able to:

- Identify sources of finance for business start-ups and for established businesses
- Explain short-term sources of finance available
- Explain long-term sources of finance available.

What are Sources of Finance?

- Sources of finance are *where* a business can obtain money from.
- Sources of finances assist with business start up.
- Sources of finances assist with operating costs, e.g. salaries, supplies, electricity bills.
- Sources of finance help with the expansion costs of a business, e.g. investing in new technologies.

Short-term Finance

- **Short-term sources of finance** are for small amounts of borrowing, which must be repaid within one year.
- There are different types of short-term finance:

> **Key Point**
>
> Overdrafts tend to be on a variable rate of interest, which means if the Bank of England decides to raise the bank base rate, businesses have to pay more interest on any borrowing they have on overdrafts.

Short-term finance option	Explained	Advantages	Disadvantages
Overdraft facility	An **overdraft** is when a bank allows a business to withdraw more money than it has in its account and pay it back later.	Quick, convenient, flexible; interest paid only on the amount of money borrowed and for the amount of time it is borrowed.	High, variable rates of interest; a bank may not grant the facility and can remove it at any time.
Trade credit	**Trade credit** is when a business receives goods from a supplier immediately but agrees to pay for them later.	A business receives payment from customers before paying suppliers, removing the need to raise its own finance.	Not all suppliers offer trade credit; suppliers might charge a higher selling price. New businesses may not be offered trade credit until financial trust is gained.

Long-term Finance

- **Long-term sources of finance** tend to be for larger amounts of money that are needed for longer periods of time, e.g. for start-up purposes or for business expansion. There are different types of long-term finance – see the next page for details.

Long-term finance option	Explained	Advantages	Disadvantages
Personal savings	Personal savings are the owner's own money.	Quick and easy to obtain; no interest. Maintain the same level of ownership and control of the business.	Might need the money for personal reasons. Might not want to risk losing the money.
Retained profits	Retained profit is profit made and kept from previous trading years.	Quick and easy to obtain; no interest. Maintain the same level of ownership and control of the business.	Might need the money for other needs; might not have any retained profit (especially if a new business).
Venture capital	Experienced business people with large capital offer venture capital to invest.	Large capital sums; no need to repay; no interest; risk carried by venture capitalists; business advice and experience offered.	Loss of control of decisions; profit is shared; may cause conflict with existing shareholders.
Share capital	Share capital is when a business owner sells shares in the business.	No need to repay; no interest. Private limited companies can retain as much control as possible by inviting family and friends to buy shares. Public limited companies can benefit from this quick way to raise significant capital.	Profit is shared; may cause conflict with existing shareholders; loss of control; financial information becomes public. For private limited companies, finding investors might be difficult; for public limited companies, greater public scrutiny of business performance. For public limited companies, there is loss of control in the business and financial data becomes public.
Bank loan	A loan is a sum of money lent by a bank to a business to repay in monthly repayments.	Business retains control over business; does not have to share profits; fixed loan repayments, so if interest rates increase, loan repayments will remain the same.	Takes time to arrange; interest is charged; bank might not grant loan; inflexible as repayments must be made on time. Collateral is often required (which is something valuable pledged by the business as security if the business fails to make its repayments).
Crowdfunding	An online appeal made to attract multiple investors who wish to put in small amounts each (crowdfunding).	Risk is shared amongst many; no interest; can reach a wide number of investors; acts as a method of promotion; a good way of testing a business idea; does not need to be repaid.	If the overall target funds are not reached, finance is returned to investors; the reputation of the business may suffer if fundraising fails; a business idea may be copied by anyone who sees it on the Internet; profits are shared.
Sale of assets	When a business sells an item of value, it is a sale of assets.	No interest; easy and convenient; creates valuable space.	Assets may not realise full market price or not sell at all; can be seen as a desperate measure; may regret selling assets that are needed in the future.

Quick Test

1. Define the terms 'short-term finance' and 'long-term finance'.
2. Explain **one** benefit of trade credit to a business.
3. Define the term 'overdraft'.

Key Words

short-term sources of finance
overdraft
trade credit
long-term sources of finance
personal savings
retained profit

venture capital
share capital
loan
crowdfunding
sale of assets

1 Which **two** of the following are examples of customer needs?
Select **two** answers.   [2]

A Lifestyle ☐

B Quality ☐

C Choice ☐

D Age ☐

E Advertising ☐

2 Explain **one** reason why businesses must anticipate customer needs.   [3]

3 Explain **one** purpose of market research when starting a new business.   [3]

4 Give **two** benefits to a business of providing goods and services that customers want. [2]

5 Define the term 'secondary market research'.   [1]

6 Give **two** examples of how a business can collect qualitative data. [2]

_____

_____

7 Define the term 'market segmentation'. [1]

_____

_____

8 Explain **one** purpose of market mapping. [3]

_____

_____

_____

_____

9 Give **one** disadvantage of market mapping. [1]

_____

_____

10 Which **two** of the following are examples of how businesses compete?
Select **two** answers. [2]

A Location ☐

B Legislation ☐

C Debts ☐

D Name ☐

E Product range ☐

11 Give **one** method that a business can use to gain a competitive advantage. [1]

_____

_____

1. Which **one** of the following is considered to be a fixed cost?
   Select **one** answer. [1]

   A Raw materials ☐   C Insurance ☐

   B Packaging ☐   D Overtime wages ☐

2. Explain **one** financial objective of a business. [3]

   ....

   ....

   ....

3. The table below shows the financial information of a small business for one month.

Sales quantity	Selling price	Variable cost per unit	Fixed cost
1000	£15	£5	£5000

   a) Using the information above, calculate the break-even point for the small business.
      You are advised to show your workings. [2]

      ....

      ....

   b) Using the information above, calculate the margin of safety for the small business.
      You are advised to show your workings. [2]

      ....

      ....

4. Which **two** of the following are examples of variable costs?
   Select **two** answers. [2]

   A Raw materials ☐   D Salaries ☐

   B Rent ☐   E Wages of staff that produce
                                 goods and services ☐

   C Advertising ☐

5. Give **one** example of a cash outflow. [1]

   ....

6 Explain **one** long-term source of finance. [3]

....

....

....

7 Explain **one** short-term source of finance. [3]

....

....

....

....

8 The table below shows the interest of a loan for a small business for one year.

| Amount borrowed | £15 000 |
| Amount repaid | £16 000 |

Using the information above, calculate the interest rate percentage for the loan.
You are advised to show your workings. [2]

....

....

9 Explain **one** limitation of using share capital as a source of finance. [3]

....

....

....

....

10 Explain **one** reason why cash is important to a business. [3]

....

....

....

....

The Options for Start-ups and Small Businesses

You must be able to:

- Discuss the concept of limited liability
- Explain the advantages and disadvantages of different types of business ownership
- Discuss the option of starting up and running a franchise operation.

Liability

- **Liability** is the legal responsibility that a business owner has to pay his/her business's debts.
- The two types of liability are **limited liability** and **unlimited liability**.
- An entrepreneur needs to think about the risk of liability when considering types of business ownership.

Limited Liability

- There is a legal difference between the business owner and the business, meaning that owners have limited liability.
- If the business incurs debts, they belong to the business. Owners will only lose the money they have invested in the business.
- A **private limited company (Ltd)** has limited liability.

Unlimited Liability

- There is no legal difference between the owner and the business – the business owner is the business.
- The owner is legally responsible for the actions of the business and the business's debts – this is unlimited liability.
- If the business has debts, the owner may need to sell their personal belongings to pay the debts.
- **Business ownership** types that have unlimited liability: **sole trader** and **partnerships**.

> **Key Point**
>
> Unlimited liability means owners can lose personal possessions if their business has debts. Limited liability reduces the risk faced by owners as debts will belong to the business, not the owner.

Sole Trader

- The business is owned by one owner who has full control, although people can be employed as workers.
- The owner has unlimited liability.
- Sole trader businesses are often small, e.g. a tutor, a photographer, a social media manager.

Advantages
• Easy to set up – no fees
• Owner keeps all profits
• The owner is their own boss (self-employed)
• Decisions can be made quickly
• It is not a legal requirement to file accounts

Disadvantages
• Personal belongings are at risk (unlimited liability)
• Difficult to raise money
• Earnings are lost if the owner is sick or takes a holiday
• Profits are taxed as income so if the business makes high profits, the tax amount is increased
• The owner may have to work across all areas of the business (e.g. finance and marketing) and this may be stressful

Partnership

- A partnership is a business usually owned by 2 to 20 people.
- Partners share control and decision making. Important information (e.g. profit split) is set out in the 'deed of partnership' – a document agreed by the partners.
- There is unlimited liability for all partners unless they set up a Limited Liability Partnership (LLP) where partners will only be liable for what they have invested.
- Many professional services are set up as partnerships, e.g. doctors' surgery, dentists, vets, solicitors.

Advantages
• More capital can be raised by partners
• Partners can bring a range of skills
• It is not a legal requirement to file accounts
• Problems and decisions are shared
• Responsibility for debt is shared

Disadvantages
• Unlimited liability (unless a Limited Liability Partnership)
• Partners may have disagreements
• Profits are shared
• If a partner dies or becomes bankrupt, the partnership will have to close

Private Limited Company

- A business that can have multiple owners. The owners are called shareholders as they own a portion (share) of the business. Only those that are invited can buy shares.
- Shareholders need to register the business as a company (incorporation) with Companies House and have 'Ltd' after their name.
- A tax is paid on profits; this is called corporation tax.
- The shareholders each have unlimited liability.
- Entrepreneurs can set up any business as a private limited company, e.g. videographers for social media content.

Advantages
• Limited liability
• People can be invited to buy shares to raise money
• As shareholders must be invited, there is less risk of a takeover

Disadvantages
• It is a legal requirement to file the company's accounts, and this is available for anyone to view, including competitors
• More administration involved to get started as a private limited company; this is time consuming

Franchising

- A franchise is an arrangement between an established business (the franchisor) that allows an entrepreneur or business (franchisee/s) the right to sell goods and services using its name, trademark and business processes, e.g. Subway.
- An entrepreneur or business (franchisee) buying into the franchise operates as an independent business.
- A fee is paid to start as a franchise. A percentage of profits, known as royalties, is also paid by the franchisee to the franchisor.

Advantages to the franchisee
• The brand and customer base is already established
• A high chance the business will be successful
• Support and training is provided by the franchisor, e.g. marketing and staff training

Disadvantages to the franchisee
• Start-up fees can be expensive
• Franchisor must be paid a percentage of the profits
• Little control and flexibility – products are already created and decisions made
• Complicated application process

Quick Test

1. List the start-up options that have unlimited liability.
2. Give three disadvantages of being a sole trader.
3. Define the term 'franchising'.

Key Words

liability	business ownership	Companies House
limited liability	sole trader	franchise
unlimited liability	partnership	franchisor
private limited company (Ltd)	shareholders	franchisee
	incorporation	

Business Location

You must be able to:

- Discuss the factors that influence business location
- Explain how the Internet has made an impact on location decisions for businesses.

Choosing a Business Location

- **Business location** is the place where a business operates.
- For some businesses, location is very important. Customers need them to be in a convenient place, so they can travel there easily and regularly, e.g. a barber's shop.
- Some small businesses do not need a physical location and can set up and run online.

The right location for a business will depend on the nature of the business and the desired proximity with respect to:
- market
- labour
- materials
- competitors.

Proximity to Market

- Market is the people buying the goods and services. For some businesses, customers need easy access to purchase their products.
- A convenience store will want to be local to customers but this is not so important for a luxury jewellery designer as people will be prepared to travel there.

Proximity to Labour

- Labour is the people that work for a business or that the business may want to employ.
- Businesses will need to be in an area that has enough suitably skilled staff willing to work at the salary/wages on offer.

Proximity to Materials

- Materials are the items used to make products.
- For a bulk-gaining product (the final product is larger than the **raw materials**), it is better to be located close to the market, as it will be expensive to transport the larger end product (e.g. it is easier to transport car parts than a car).
- For a bulk-reducing product (the final product is smaller than the raw materials), it is better to be located near to the raw materials (e.g. it will be more expensive to transport potatoes than packets of crisps).

Proximity to Competitors
- Some businesses locate near to competitors to provide choice to customers (e.g. restaurants in a food court).
- Other businesses will not want to compete for buyers so will locate further from similar businesses (e.g. a car wash).

Nature of Business

- The nature of the business refers to the business activities, the type of business and which sector the business operates in.
- Businesses in the **primary sector** (acquiring raw materials) need to be where the raw materials are located. For example, a farmer will need to locate somewhere with lots of land to grow vegetables or keep animals.
- Businesses in the **secondary sector** (manufacturing and assembly) will need to be in areas where transport links are good so that supplies can be brought in and sent out with ease.
- Businesses in the **tertiary sector** (commercial services) will want to be located close to or within easy access to customers. For example, a hotel will want to be close to attractions or transport links.

Impact of the Internet on Location Decisions

- The Internet has now made it easier for some businesses to get started without the need for business premises.
- Businesses can use the Internet to complete transactions called **e-commerce**. Transactions through smartphones are called **m-commerce** and transactions through social media are called **social commerce**.
- The marketplace (where buyers and sellers meet) can be online so a business does not need to be located close to customers. For example, freelancers can sell their professional services through sites such as Fiverr.

> **Key Point**
>
> The Internet has made it easier to set up and run a business as physical location is less important than the goods and services being sold.

> **Quick Test**
>
> 1. List **three** factors that a business needs to consider when deciding its location.
> 2. Give **one** reason why locating near competitors may be a good idea.
> 3. Give **one** impact the Internet has had on location.

> **Key Words**
>
> business location
> raw materials
> primary sector
> secondary sector
> tertiary sector
> e-commerce
> m-commerce
> social commerce

Quick Recall Quiz

The Marketing Mix

You must be able to:

- Define the marketing mix and understand the importance of each element
- Explain the importance of a balanced marketing mix to operate in a competitive environment
- Explain how changing consumer needs impact the marketing mix
- Discuss the impact of technology on the marketing mix.

Elements of the Marketing Mix

- The **marketing mix** is a combination of four factors a business must consider to meet customer needs, known as the 4Ps: price, product, promotion and place.
- The elements of the marketing mix complement each other and a business needs to get the right balance across the 4Ps to attract customers (e.g. high-quality materials used for a product with a high selling price).
- The marketing mix is different for each business and changes over time.

Price

- The price is the amount customers must pay for goods or services.
- A business should set a price that it knows customers are willing to pay.
- Price can be used to attract new customers (e.g. a low price may increase sales as it is cheaper for customers).

Product

- The product is what the business is selling. It can be a good or a service and this must meet customer needs.
- An entrepreneur will want their product to be different to that of competitors; this can be achieved by creating a unique selling point (e.g. creating a viral promotional video).

Promotion

- Promotion creates awareness, boosts sales, builds a brand and communicates the features of a product.
- Small businesses may use social media adverts or influencers. Other methods of promotion include email messages that advertise special offers.

Place

- Place is about how the product reaches customers – where and when they want it.
- A business can sell directly, through the Internet or from a business premise.
- Another selling option is through **retailers** or **wholesalers**.

> **Key Point**
>
> The marketing mix is the combination of price, product, promotion and place.

Balancing the Marketing Mix

- The competitive environment of a business determines which element of the marketing mix is most important.
- If a business operates in a mass market (meaning there are many different businesses offering the same product), a low price or special discounts may be used to set them apart from competitors.
- Having a user-friendly website or many delivery options helps to make a business competitive using the 'place' element of the marketing mix.
- Modifying each element in the marketing mix establishes a differentiated product, enabling a business to be competitive.
- A business has to conduct research to stay up to date with the needs of customers and make adjustments to the marketing mix.
- When a new product is introduced, the marketing mix will be different to when the product is established and the brand has grown.

Technology and the Marketing Mix

- Changes in technology, e.g. e-commerce and **digital communication**, affect the marketing mix.

- **Place** – a small business can build a large customer base through selling online – it can target customers anywhere in the world and doesn't need to have physical premises.
- **Promotion** – digital communication, available through websites, email and social media gives businesses new promotion opportunities. A web-banner can be placed on multiple websites at a fraction of the cost of a billboard poster.
- **Price** – customers have more access to information; this makes them more knowledgeable about prices through comparison websites, so some businesses may have to change their prices to remain competitive. A business may be able to lower prices due to cost savings made from using technology in the production process.
- **Product** – social media and online customer reviews allow businesses to conduct market research and get first-hand comments from customers to identify how to meet their needs.

Key Point

The competitive environment of a business determines which element of the marketing mix is most important.

Quick Test

1. Give the element of the marketing mix which involves communicating the features of a product.
2. Give **one** way in which operating in a competitive environment will impact a business's marketing mix.
3. Give **one** way in which technology has made an impact on the price element of the marketing mix.

Key Words

marketing mix
retailer
wholesaler
digital communication

Business Plans

You must be able to:

- State the elements a business plan contains
- Explain the role and importance of a business plan.

What is a Business Plan?

- A **business plan** is a document prepared by entrepreneurs, which summarises the future objectives of the proposed business and shows how they will be achieved.
- Entrepreneurs use a business plan to review all areas of the business. It is also used by banks and venture capitalists to assess if the business is likely to be successful before lending money.

What does a Business Plan Contain?

The Business Idea

- A simple description of the purpose of the business and why the business will be a success.

Business Aims and Objectives

- The long-term goals of the business and the medium- to short-term steps to get there.

Target Market

- The group of people that the business will sell to. Through market research a customer profile can be created.

Forecast Revenue, Cost and Profit

- Predictions for how much the business will make from selling its goods or services, its costs and potential profit.

Cash-flow Forecast

- Monthly inflows and outflows of the business. An entrepreneur can see when cash-flow may be negative and think about borrowing money to cover these times.

Sources of Finance

- The amount of money required to start a business and where it will come from (including money invested by the entrepreneur, how much will need to be borrowed and when).

Location

- The business's location and specific information about the area. Also what the business will need to set up in this location.

Marketing Mix

- Each element of the marketing mix will need to be explained.

Why is it Important to Have a Business Plan?

- Banks and other investors will want to see a business plan to determine whether the business has a good chance of being successful.
- Potential investors will look at the financial information to ensure the business will be able to pay back any money that is borrowed with interest.
- Writing a business plan forces entrepreneurs to think about every aspect of the business – this may highlight areas that need further consideration.
- It is a plan that entrepreneurs can refer to and ensure there is direction for the business.
- Costly mistakes can be avoided if the business is well planned out, e.g. if an entrepreneur is aware of the costs of raw materials, they can carefully budget and set prices accordingly.
- The legal responsibilities of the business can be researched and planned for using a business plan.
- The risk of failure is reduced if the business has a plan and clear aims and objectives.
- Although business plans are important, not all entrepreneurs write one, preferring instead to go with their gut instinct.

> **Key Point**
>
> A business plan is important to minimise the risk of failure and to help obtain finance.

> **Quick Test**
>
> 1. List the essential elements of a business plan.
> 2. Give **one** stakeholder who would be interested in seeing a business plan.
> 3. Give **one** way in which a business plan helps to reduce the risk of a business failing.

> **Key Word**
>
> business plan

1 Explain **one** reason why survival may be a more appropriate objective for a new business rather than an existing one. [3]

2 Explain **one** objective of a social enterprise. [3]

3 Identify **two** variable costs of a business that produces chocolate. [2]

4 Explain **one** reason why a business may become insolvent. [3]

5 Identify **two** long-term sources of finance. [2]

6 The table shows the financial information of a small business for one month.

Sales quantity	18000
Selling price	£8
Variable cost per unit	£4
Fixed cost	£10000

a) Using the information above, calculate the break-even point for the small business. You are advised to show your workings. [2]

b) Using the information above, calculate the margin of safety for the small business. You are advised to show your workings. [2]

c) Using the information above, calculate the profit for the small business. You are advised to show your workings. [2]

7 Explain **one** benefit of using retained profit as a source of finance. [3]

8 Explain **one** limitation of using trade credit as a source of finance. [3]

1 Define the term 'sole trader'. [1]

2 Explain **one** disadvantage of operating as a sole trader. [3]

3 Give **one** benefit of choosing to start up a partnership. [1]

4 Which **two** of the following are factors that affect business location?
Select **two** answers. [2]

A The minimum wage ☐   D Materials ☐

B Income tax ☐   E Interest rates ☐

C Labour ☐

5 Give **one** reason why location is important for businesses in the primary sector. [1]

6 Give **one** reason why a business may choose a location close to labour. [1]

7 Which **two** of the following are elements of the marketing mix?
Select **two** answers. [2]

A Product ☐   D Promotion ☐

B Purchase ☐   E Planning ☐

C Profitability ☐

8 Define the term 'place'. [1]

....

....

9 Explain **one** impact technology has made on the place element of the marketing mix. [3]

....

....

....

....

10 Give **one** purpose of a business plan. [1]

....

....

11 Which **two** of the following items will be included in a business plan?
Select **two** answers. [2]

A Design mix ☐ **D** Product life cycle ☐

B Aims and objectives ☐ **E** A list of all staff ☐

C Cash-flow forecast ☐

12 Explain **one** advantage of having a business plan. [3]

....

....

....

....

....

Business Stakeholders

You must be able to:

- Identify who business stakeholders are and their different objectives
- Understand the role of stakeholders in a small business and how they can impact on the business
- Explain how stakeholders can often experience conflict.

What is a Stakeholder?

- A **stakeholder** is:
  - any person who has an interest in a business
  - any person who is affected by the activities of a business
  - any person who works for a business
  - any person who supplies a business
  - any person who competes with a business
  - any person who lives in the neighbourhood of a business
  - pressure groups who campaign against the activities of a business
  - any person who buys from a business or is the **end user** of its products.
- Internal stakeholders are people inside the business such as owners, management and employees.
- External stakeholders are people outside the business such as customers, suppliers and **banks**.

Internal Stakeholders

- **Owners** want profits, a good reputation and the potential to grow the business.
- **Managers** want good salaries, recognition for achieving targets and career success.
- **Employees** want good working conditions, a decent wage and job security.

External Stakeholders

- Shareholders want a return on their investment in **dividend** payouts.
- **Suppliers** want to sell their products at the highest price and be paid on time.
- **Customers** want to buy quality and reliable goods and services at the lowest price.
- The **local community** wants local investment, jobs and limited pollution.
- **Government** wants low unemployment, competitive markets, and businesses to operate within the law and pay taxes.
- Banks want to lend money to businesses with limited risk of losing it.
- **Pressure groups** want to ensure businesses are acting ethically and are not polluting the environment.

> **Key Point**
>
> Do not confuse **stake**holders with **share**holders.

The Influence of Stakeholders

- Stakeholders can both influence a business or be influenced by the activities of a business.
- Owners make decisions that can influence the success of their business, e.g. deciding to open a new shop to expand the business: choosing the right location is critical.
- Employees can influence a business by providing excellent customer service, which helps to boost the brand image of the business. On the other hand, staff with poor customer service skills can drive away customers.
- Suppliers can influence a business by supplying it with goods of excellent quality, which can lead to repeat purchase by the business's customers. However, if supplies are of poor, or even dangerous quality, customers may choose in the future to buy goods elsewhere so the business and its suppliers lose custom.

Stakeholder Conflict

- Often stakeholders have different aims, which can cause **stakeholder conflict**, causing them to pull in different directions.
- This is because stakeholders do not always make decisions which are in the best interests of a business, instead they often aim to satisfy their own interests.

For example:

- The owner of a business may want to pay its workers the lowest wages in order to keep costs down so that customers can benefit from lower prices.
- However, if workers are paid low wages they are more likely to be dissatisfied, which might lead to low productivity, poor quality of work and increased labour turnover.
- Therefore the business owner will need to balance the needs of profit with the desire for quality, motivated staff; some form of compromise will need to be made which best satisfies the owner, customers and workers.

Key Point

Stakeholders may have conflicting interests.

Key Words

stakeholders
end user
bank
owners
managers
employees
dividend
suppliers
customers
local community
government
pressure groups
stakeholder conflict

Technology and Business

Quick Recall Quiz

You must be able to:

- Explain different types of technology used by businesses
- Explain how technology influences business activity.

Technology and Sales

- Technology has brought e-commerce, which is buying and selling goods and services online.
- E-commerce makes it possible for businesses to sell at any time of day, so businesses can make continuous **sales**.
- E-commerce has made it possible for businesses to attract a wider target audience from around the world.
- E-commerce has created a larger marketplace for businesses, which has helped increase sales.
- Technology has brought new **payment systems** (the electronic ability to transfer money quickly and safely from one bank account to another) such as PayPal, bringing time efficiency for customers.
- Businesses are now able to take orders online and deliver goods to customers' homes in a very short period of time.

> ### Key Point
>
> Technology has provided businesses with more opportunities to sell to customers. It has also made business more competitive with prices.

Technology and Costs

- Keeping **costs** to a minimum is vital for any business and through the use of technology, businesses are now able to compare the prices of suppliers quickly and easily to identify the cheapest suppliers.
- Many business start-ups use e-commerce without the need to find physical premises; this helps reduce overheads.
- To create a website and PayPal account is cheap and simple, so it is possible for one person to open and run a business without the need to hire technical staff.
- New technologies tend to remove the need for old machinery, or even human work, which has reduced costs, e.g.
  - Amazon relies more on robots in its warehouses than human workers
  - It is possible for Amazon's robots to function on a 24-hour basis, which humans are unable to do, thus reducing Amazon's operational costs.
- Businesses now use **digital communication** such as emails, texts and websites to communicate with different stakeholders; this is quick, efficient and cheap.
- Many businesses use **biometrics** to reduce time and increase efficiency and security, e.g. fingerprint scanning, iris scanning.

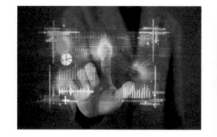

Technology and the Marketing Mix

- The marketing mix is a blend of the 4Ps: product, place, price and promotion.

Product

- Businesses are becoming more innovative with goods and services to keep up with changes in technology, e.g. streaming platforms like Disney+ and Netflix.
- Some goods have revolutionised certain industries, e.g. digital photography and Instagram.
- Some services have been created thanks to technology, e.g. Uber spotted an opportunity to use apps to bring customers and drivers together to remove the need for traditional taxi firms in some cities.
- In order to keep pace with technology and consumer demand, businesses have to continue innovating their goods and services.

Place

- Before e-commerce, business activities were more restricted – to buy goods and services, customers needed to visit shops.
- Shops have restricted opening hours, which meant customers could only buy goods and services when the shops were open.
- Websites are fast becoming the new 'place' to trade.
- Smartphones provide customers with portable access to the Internet, enabling them to instantly buy products.

Price

- Technology has brought more efficiency in costs and time, enabling some businesses to cut the prices of the goods they sell.
- Customers can now compare prices using price-comparison websites, which in turn has encouraged businesses to reduce prices in order to remain competitive.

Promotion

- Technology has made promotion quicker and cheaper for many businesses due to advancements in communication such as texts, emails and video calling, e.g. Skype.
- Social media provides an effective way of promoting products via online campaigns. This also includes the use of paid advertisements to influencers who have many followers.
- **Viral marketing** encourages consumers and the public to use social media to share information about a business's goods and services, e.g Netflix.

> ### Key Point
>
> Technology affects all areas of the marketing mix: product, place, price and promotion.

> ### Key Words
>
> sales
> payment systems
> costs
> digital communication
> biometrics
> viral marketing

> ### Quick Test
>
> 1. Define the term 'e-commerce'.
> 2. Give **one** way in which technology can influence prices.
> 3. Give **one** way in which technology can influence the marketing mix.

Legislation and Business

You must be able to:

- Explain the purpose of legislation
- Discuss the impact that employment legislation and consumer legislation has on business.

Legislation, and Why it is Important

- **Legislation** refers to laws set by governments of countries.
- Legislation sets out a strict set of rules in which businesses can operate that do not exploit staff or customers.
- No business can gain a cost advantage over another by avoiding implementing costly requirements due to legislation; therefore, legislation is fair to all businesses.

The Principles of Employment Law

- All workers are entitled to be free of **discrimination** in the workplace.
- Businesses must treat all job applicants and workers fairly regardless of gender, age, race, religion, disability, sexual preference, type of contract or stage of pregnancy.
- All workers are entitled to receive a minimum wage. The National Living Wage is slightly higher than the minimum wage. Without this legislation, it would be possible for businesses to pay workers as little as the business wanted.
- All workers are protected from working too many hours each week.
- Any worker with a young family is entitled to time off work to look after their family.
- The Health and Safety Act states all workers have the right to work in a safe environment.
- Businesses examine all work areas to ensure no member of staff comes to harm (known as risk assessment).
- If a business needs to reduce its staffing levels, it must provide staff with sufficient warning and pay them compensation (redundancy pay).

> **Key Point**
>
> You will not have to learn the names of specific laws but you will need to know the purpose of legislation and the impact it has on business.

The Principles of Consumer Law

- A **customer** is anyone who *buys* a product.
- **Consumers** are people who *use* products.
- The Consumer Rights Act states the right to a refund if goods or services are not:

a) **of satisfactory quality** – which means that goods or services shouldn't be faulty or damaged when the consumer receives them.
  - Goods should last a 'reasonable' length of time.
  - Customers don't have the right to a refund if they damage the goods themselves or knew about existing damage at the point of sale.

b) **fit for purpose** – which means the goods or service must be able to do what they were designed to do.

c) **as described** – which means the description must match the product being sold.

- Goods and services must be correctly packaged and clearly labelled with correct measurements so customers are not deceived by any description.
- However, customers do not have a right to a refund if the goods or services are described correctly but a customer changes their mind after they have made the purchase.

Business and Complying with the Law

- If a business is caught breaking the law, it is likely to be heavily fined.
- If a business is caught breaking the law the owners or key staff may also be given prison sentences.
- By complying with the law businesses can avoid financial penalties or jail sentences.
- If customers learn of a business breaking the law, they may be disgusted and decide to never shop there again, which will affect future sales.
- A business should want to obey the law in order to maintain a strong brand image in the long term, which helps future sales.

Changes in legislation

Quick Test

1. Define the term 'legislation'.
2. List **two** areas of employment law that a business must comply with.
3. List **three** areas of consumer law that businesses need to obey.

Key Words

legislation
discrimination
customer
consumer

The Economy and Business

You must be able to:

- Understand the impact of the economic climate on business
- Discuss how changing levels of income affect consumer spending
- Analyse the impact various economic factors can have on a business.

Economic Climate

- **Economic climate** refers to the broad performance of an economy.
- The economy is measured by **Gross Domestic Product (GDP)**, which is an estimate of the total value of goods and services produced in a country.
- The more the country produces, the stronger the economy is, and the healthier the economic climate.

Changing Levels of Consumer Income

- **Consumer income** is the amount of money consumers have left to spend after they have paid their taxes and living expenses.
- When consumer income rises, people tend to have more money, which leads to higher levels of **consumer spending**.
- Consumers tend to buy more expensive goods and services (luxuries) when they have lots of money.
- When consumer income reduces, people are not earning as much money so may spend less money or buy cheaper (inferior) products.

Unemployment and Business

- **Unemployment** has different impacts on the economy.

When unemployment is low	When unemployment is high
More workers are employed.	There are not enough jobs for people who are willing to work.
People have higher consumer income.	People have less consumer income.
Consumers spend more money.	Consumers spend less money.
Demand for luxury goods and services increases.	Demand for inferior goods and services increases.
Businesses produce more luxury products.	Businesses produce more inferior products.
Businesses hire more staff.	Businesses stop hiring and begin to make workers redundant.
There is a shortage of quality staff.	There is a surplus of quality staff.
Increased revenue and profit for businesses.	Decreased revenue and profit for businesses.
The government receives more tax and pays out less in benefits.	The government receives less tax and pays out more in benefits.

Other Factors that Affect Businesses and Consumer Income

Factor	Definition	When high	When low
Corporation Tax	A tax government charges to businesses based on a percentage of their profits.	Business costs increase and prices tend to increase.	Business costs decrease and prices tend to decrease.
Value Added Tax (VAT)	A tax added on top of selling prices for goods and services (or businesses whose turnover is more than £85 000 (2023)).	The price of goods and services increases.	The price of goods and services decreases.
Income Tax	A tax paid to the government by individuals, based on their annual income.	Less consumer income.	More consumer income.
Inflation	**Inflation** is when the prices of goods and services continue to rise.	Higher costs for businesses and higher prices for consumers.	Lower costs for businesses and lower prices for consumers.
Interest rates (charged by banks as a result of the Bank Base Rate set by the Bank of England)	The cost of borrowing (and reward for saving) money is the **interest rate**.	The cost of borrowing increases for businesses and consumers, so their costs increase.	The cost of borrowing decreases for businesses and consumers, so their costs decrease.
Exchange rates	The cost of exchanging one currency for another is the **exchange rate**.	When the pound is high, imports are cheap (meaning more consumer income), exports are expensive.	When the pound is low, imports are expensive (meaning less consumer income), exports are cheap.

Quick Test

1. Define the term 'economic climate'.
2. Explain **one** way in which unemployment affects businesses.
3. Define the term 'interest rate'.

External Influences

You must be able to:

- Understand the importance of external influences on a business
- Analyse the possible responses to changes in technology, legislation and the economic climate.

Business Responses to Changes in Technology

- Many businesses now use computer-aided manufacturing (CAM), robots and 3D printing to replace or assist human labour.
- Shops and other provider services, such as restaurants, have Electronic Funds Transfer at Point of Sale (EFTPOS), which speeds up transactions. EFTPOS also provides vital electronic data to help businesses maintain stock levels.
- Technology has changed the workplace as staff use more emails, video calls and websites.
- Technology is also being used for marketing purposes and many businesses recruit and train staff for telemarketing, which involves servicing and selling products to customers over the telephone.
- Businesses and customers can interact through social media comments, likes and polls.

The Pros and Cons of Technology

- Technology has helped reduce running costs and wastage whilst increasing productivity, competitiveness, innovation, speed and accuracy.
- Technology costs money to buy and install, to train staff to use, and to maintain and replace.
- Technology has been criticised for job losses, loss of traditional skills and the demotivation of staff.

Legislation and Regulation

Legislation and regulation	Purpose
Employment laws	To ensure workers: work in a safe environment; receive fair wages; are treated equally; do not work too many hours; are treated fairly if made redundant.
Consumer Rights Act	The Consumer Rights Act is a law that protects consumer rights when buying products from businesses.
Trading Standards Authority (TSA)	The Trading Standards Authority (TSA) is a local government service that regulates and enforces to ensure the public is protected from businesses selling counterfeits (fakes), inaccurate measures and inaccurate weights of goods.

Advertising Standards Authority (ASA)	The Advertising Standards Authority (ASA) is the UK's independent advertising regulator that ensures all business advertising is accurate and true. It also deals with complaints from the public about advertising.
Environmental laws	Minimise risk to the environment and to the health of the public.
Tax laws	Ensure businesses are paying the correct taxes to the government.
Competition law	To ensure no businesses becomes dominant and that prices are fair.

Impact of the Economic Environment

- **Exchange rates** have a large impact on businesses that import or export.
- The acronym **SPICED** is useful to help remember:
  - when there is a **S**trong **P**ound, **I**mports are **C**heap, and **E**xports are **D**ear.
- **Interest rates** affect businesses too.
- When interest rates are high, businesses often find costs go up as it becomes expensive to borrow.
- When interest rates are high, businesses are less likely to invest.
- When interest rates are high, consumers with mortgages, loans and credit cards tend to have less income, so reduce their spending, which means fewer sales for businesses.
- When interest rates are low, consumers tend to have more money to spend.
- **Inflation** means a rise in prices.
- Inflation tends to be bad for business as it increases costs for businesses, reducing profits, unless businesses pass these costs on to their customers (which may lead to fewer sales).
- **Unemployment** affects the whole of business and society.
- When there is high unemployment, workers have less income, which means they are less likely to spend money.
- If workers buy less, businesses sell less, which can lead to some businesses struggling as their revenue declines (perhaps resulting in more redundancies).
- **Uncertainty** in the economic outlook affects consumers and businesses, e.g. the 2016 Brexit result will have an impact for years while the government, businesses and the UK public work out how leaving the European Union affects everyone.

Key Point

Strong

Pound

Imports

Cheap

Exports

Dear

Quick Test

1. Give **one** way in which technology has changed the workplace.
2. Explain the role of the Trading Standards Authority.
3. Define the term 'inflation'.

Key Words

employment laws
Consumer Rights Act
Trading Standards Authority (TSA)
Advertising Standards Authority (ASA)
environmental laws
tax laws
competition law

1 Give **one** disadvantage of setting up as a franchise. [1]

_____

_____

2 Define the term 'liability'. [1]

_____

_____

3 Give **two** disadvantages of starting a private limited company. [2]

_____

_____

_____

4 Give **one** advantage of locating close to competitors. [1]

_____

_____

5 Explain **one** advantage the Internet has had on business location. [3]

_____

_____

_____

_____

6 Explain **one** impact to businesses of pricing their products too high. [3]

_____

_____

_____

_____

7 Explain **one** impact customers' needs have on the marketing mix. [3]

8 Give **one** advantage the Internet has had on promotion. [1]

9 Define the term 'business plan'. [1]

10 Explain **one** benefit of including a cash-flow forecast in a business plan. [3]

11 Give **one** reason why banks and lenders have an interest in a business plan. [1]

1 Which **one** of the following is an example of an internal stakeholder?
Select **one** answer. [1]

A Employees ☐ C Pressure groups ☐

B Government ☐ D Suppliers ☐

2 Which **one** of the following is **not** an external influence of a business?
Select **one** answer. [1]

A Technology ☐ C The promotion strategies of the business ☐

B Legislation ☐ D The economic climate ☐

3 Explain **one** way in which stakeholders can impact on business activity. [3]

4 Explain **one** impact that a higher unemployment rate has on a business. [3]

5 Explain **one** impact of an increase in the value of pound sterling (£) on a business that imports raw materials from abroad. [3]

6 Explain **one** consequence of not following employment law for a business. [3]

7 Which **two** of the following are examples of objectives of most businesses?
Select **two** answers. [2]

A   To make a profit ☐

B   To provide goods and services ☐

C   To sell at low prices ☐

D   To make cheap products ☐

E   To choose to remain a small business ☐

8 Give **two** basic rights of consumer law. [2]

....

....

9 Explain **one** advantage of following consumer law. [3]

....

....

....

10 Give **two** types of technology that could be used in a business. [2]

....

....

11 Explain **one** way technology could be used to change the marketing mix of a business. [3]

....

....

....

12 Explain **one** impact the government might have on a business. [3]

....

....

....

Business Growth

You must be able to:

- Identify methods of business growth
- Know the types of business ownership for growing businesses
- Analyse the appropriateness of sources of finance for growing and established businesses.

Why Would a Business Want to Grow?

- If a business grows, it can:
  - benefit from **economies of scale**
  - which means being able to provide more goods or services, making it cheaper to make each product
  - benefit from a larger market share
  - gain more recognition, customers, revenue and profit.

Growing a Business

The following table details how to grow a business.

	Organic (internal) growth	Inorganic (external) growth
Definition	**Organic growth** is when a business grows on its own. This could be through entering new markets or creating new products.	**Inorganic growth** is when a business combines with another business to grow.

How is it achieved?	Through changing the marketing mix by:
	• Taking existing products to new markets in the UK or overseas.
	• Developing new products via:
	  – research and development
	  – taking advantage of new technology
	  – innovation.
	• Becoming a **public limited company (plc)** by floating on the stock market (see next page).
		Through a:
		• **Merger** (when two businesses join together)
		• **Takeover** (when one business buys a smaller business).

Advantages	• A business can maintain its own values without interference. • Expansion using products that are already successful reduces risk.	• Rapid growth. • New shared resources/skills/customers. • Could reduce competition by purchasing a rival.
Disadvantages	• Slower growth.	• Disagreements and communication problems.

Finance Options for Growth

- Capital found from within a business is an **internal source of finance.**
- Capital found from outside a business is an **external source of finance.**
- The table on the opposite page helps to clarify these options.

Key Point

Inorganic growth (through merger with, or takeover of, another business) can speed business expansion.

Finance options	Advantages	Disadvantages
Internal source of finance		
• **Retained profits** – using capital from profits kept from previous years of trading.	Cheap, quick and convenient.	Might not have any retained profits or might need the funds for something else. Also, once the money is gone, it's not available for future unseen problems.
• Sale of **assets**, e.g. selling machinery or land.	Convenient, can create space for more profitable uses, can be quick.	Might not get the market value or even sell at all; might need the assets in the future. It also looks desperate.
• Owner's own savings.	Quick, convenient and cheap.	Might not have any savings or may need cash for private purposes.
External source of finance		
• **Loan capital** – lump sum of capital borrowed from a bank.	Regular repayments spread over a period of time assist with cash-flow management. Often a bank manager gives financial advice.	Can take a while to be approved; might not qualify; interest applies, so can be expensive. Often a bank will insist on collateral (security) being offered by a business in case the business fails to make loan repayments.
• **Share capital** (also known as share issue) – when a business becomes a private limited company by offering shares in the business in exchange for capital.	Does not need to be repaid; no interest applies; business can choose who to offer shares to.	Profits are paid to shareholders (known as dividends); control of the business is diluted.
• **Stock market flotation** – when a business becomes a public limited company by offering shares to the public to buy.	Can raise large amounts of capital as is easy for the public to buy shares via a stockbroker or bank; does not need to be repaid; no interest applies; business becomes more recognised.	Complicated and expensive; loss of control as anyone can buy shares; profits are paid to shareholders (dividends); business records are made public; some investors only buy shares to make a quick profit by selling them when the share price increases.

Key Words

economies of scale

organic growth

inorganic growth

public limited company (plc)

merger

takeover

internal source of finance

external source of finance

retained profits

assets

loan capital

share capital

stock market flotation

Quick Test

1. Define the terms 'organic growth' and 'inorganic growth'.
2. Explain the benefits of internal finance for growth.
3. Explain the drawbacks of loan capital.

Changes in Business Aims and Objectives

Quick Recall Quiz

You must be able to:

- Explain why business aims and objectives change as businesses evolve
- Analyse how business aims and objectives change as businesses evolve.

Why Business Aims and Objectives Change as Businesses Evolve

- Aims are the long-term goals of a business.
- Objectives are the short-term steps a business takes to realise those goals.
- Over time, many businesses need to change their aims and objectives as the business evolves to adapt to changing circumstances.
- When businesses evolve, they may find **market conditions** change and they need to be able to respond to these changes, e.g. the growth rate of the market (whether the market is becoming bigger or smaller) or how competitive the market is.
- The economic climate may also have an effect on market conditions, which affects consumer income, and in turn their levels of spending.
- Consumer taste may change, e.g. an emphasis on recycling, which requires businesses to revisit their aims and objectives.
- New technology brings innovation, and businesses find they need to change their aims and objectives to remain competitive.
- Often the previous performance of a business acts as a platform for setting new aims and objectives for the future – a successful business may change its aims and objectives to include future growth or a failing business will have to revisit its aims and objectives to include a change in direction, e.g. store closures and a renewed focus on website and deliveries instead.
- **Legislation** often causes businesses to change their aims and objectives, e.g. a change in the law regarding food labelling has encouraged many businesses to adopt aims and objectives which promote public health awareness.
- Sometimes business aims and objectives change in response to internal reasons, e.g. it could be that the original aim of the business is no longer applicable. When Marks & Spencer began in 1884 it was a penny bazaar stall; now it sells a wide range of goods and services nationally and internationally.

> **Key Point**
>
> Aims and objectives change over time as the business evolves to changing circumstances.

How Aims and Objectives Change as Businesses Evolve

- Simple **survival** for a new business may change into the need to make a profit after its first year and to **growth** aims over a period of years.
- The business may have in its plans sales forecasts that require different aims and objectives for each year.
- A business may enter a new market to help it meet changed aims and objectives, e.g. Uber originally provided customers with the ability to call for transport when needed, now the business has entered the food home delivery market with UberEATS.
- Sometimes a business needs to exit a market to meet its aims and objectives, e.g. Tesco entered the American market but failed, and this failure had a negative impact on its aims and objectives, so it decided to leave the US market.
- A business may need to change the size of its workforce over time to meet changing aims and objectives, e.g. the Post Office and many seasonal stores hire extra staff over the Christmas period to cope with extra customer demand for services.
- There may be times when a business has to reduce its workforce in order to meet its changing aims and objectives.
- Sometimes businesses need to change their product range to meet changed aims and objectives, e.g. many dairy farmers now produce cheese and yogurt products in addition to milk.
- Some businesses have reduced their **product range** to return to their core business in order to meet their aims and objectives.

Key Point

As technology evolves, many businesses need to change their aims and objectives to keep up with innovation.

Quick Test

1. List **three** reasons why a business may need to change its aims and objectives.
2. List **three** ways in which aims and objectives may change as a business evolves.
3. Define the term 'survival'.

Key Words

market conditions
legislation
survival
growth
product range

Business and Globalisation

You must be able to:

- Understand the impact of globalisation on business
- Identify barriers to international trade
- Analyse how businesses compete internationally.

Globalisation and Business

- **Globalisation** is the increased integration of different economies that have increased international trade.
- **Exports** are when a business makes products in the UK then sells them to other countries.
- The UK's top exports are: pearls, gems, coins, oil and cars.
- Tourism is an export and is a major contributor to the UK economy.
- **Imports** are when products made overseas are brought into the UK.
- The top UK imports are: machines, vehicles and electronic equipment.

Changing Business Locations

- With globalisation, many UK businesses have relocated to low-cost locations overseas, e.g. Dyson vacuum cleaners are manufactured in Malaysia, where land and labour is cheaper.
- This type of relocation is known as offshoring; work is sent overseas to a host country that welcomes the operation of foreign businesses.
- Foreign businesses also locate to the UK to manufacture here, e.g. Nissan, the Japanese car company, has a plant in the UK because it wants to make the most of British skilled labour and benefit from being closer to its European customers.
- **Multinational companies (MNCs)** are businesses that operate and trade in more than one country.
- MNCs benefit from lower **production costs** by operating in developing countries and by being closer to their customers in the host countries in which they operate.
- MNCs can avoid import restrictions if they operate in host countries. Examples of MNCs are Coca-Cola and Pepsi.

Barriers to International Trade

- Many governments worry that cheap imports make it difficult for their own country's businesses to compete so they deliberately restrict opportunities, efficiency and competition for importers with **trade barriers**, such as **tariffs**.
- A tariff is a tax added onto the selling price of an imported good to make it more expensive to buy in the UK.
- If imported products are more expensive for UK consumers, they are less likely to want to buy them (reducing demand) and are more likely to buy UK products.
- If the UK imposes tariffs on imported goods, it often follows that governments of other countries also impose tariffs on UK exports entering their country, which makes it expensive for our businesses to export.
- **Trade blocs** are when certain countries group together to make it easier for members to market goods, services, capital and labour by getting rid of all barriers to trade.
- Trade blocs tend to be close to one another geographically, e.g. the North American Free Trade Agreement (NAFTA) and the European Union (EU).

How Businesses Compete Internationally

- Globalisation has created opportunities for Internet-based **e-commerce** businesses to sell to new markets; this means that businesses can use the Internet to buy and sell products anywhere in the world.
- Businesses do not even need to have their own websites or shops as they can use sites, such as eBay, to trade.
- Some businesses base their whole business model around e-commerce, such as Amazon.
- Websites even offer translation services so trading with consumers around the world becomes easier.
- Changes to the marketing mix can help a business to compete internationally, e.g. adaptation of products to suit local tastes, price amendments to take currencies into account, transportation arrangements, different promotional techniques.

> **Key Point**
>
> Tariffs are restrictions put in place by government to try to reduce cheap imports by making it more expensive and difficult for foreign countries to export to the UK.

> **Key Words**
>
> globalisation
> exports
> imports
> multinational companies (MNCs)
> production costs
> trade barriers
> tariffs
> trade blocs
> e-commerce

> **Quick Test**
>
> 1. Define the term 'globalisation'.
> 2. Define the terms 'imports' and 'exports'.
> 3. Explain how tariffs can restrict imports.

Ethics, the Environment and Business

You must be able to:

- Discuss the impact of ethical and environmental considerations on businesses
- Explain how pressure groups impact the marketing mix
- Analyse the potential trade-off between ethics and profits.

Quick Recall Quiz

What are Ethics?

- **Ethics** are moral guidelines for good behaviour – doing what is morally right.
- When a business is ethical it pays a fair wage to its workers and ensures production does not harm the environment, animals or people.

Ethics, Environmental Considerations and Trade-offs

- High profits can conflict with ethics because businesses need to produce goods and services at a cost which is less than the price it charges customers.
- Some businesses have been accused of using very cheap labour without proper health and safety provisions to minimise costs in order to make as large a profit as possible.
- Other businesses have been in the news for paying foreign suppliers who hire children to sew clothes for hours on end. This kind of negative coverage has seen customers begin to **boycott** the affected businesses in protest and a **trade-off** being needed to resolve the situation.
- Trade-offs are a compromise between one thing and another. For example, a business may spend more money checking that children are no longer used in the production of goods, or may change suppliers, in order to retain customers.
- The environment should also be protected and business activities should aim to ensure that environmental considerations are made.
- Some businesses have been accused of helping to destroy the environment, e.g. firms who use palm oil in their products. The palm oil industry burns tropical rainforests to make room for new plantations; this practice threatens the orangutan population in places like Borneo. A trade-off for such businesses would be to buy palm oil from organisations that harvest palm oil using **sustainable** methods.
- Using sustainable methods costs more, which affects profit, but ethical businesses know they need to also help the environment if they want sustainable profits.

> ### Key Point
>
> Ethical business practices can add costs to businesses. However, some businesses have found they sell more of their products by being ethical so any additional costs are outweighed by an increase in sales.

Ethics and the Reputation of a Business

- Some businesses see ethics as a form of added value to their goods and services, e.g. Lush.
- Companies who have acted in a non-ethical way have suffered criticism and drops in sales, e.g. Starbucks stores suffered when it was made public that Starbucks avoided paying UK taxes in full.

Pressure Group Activity and the Marketing Mix

- **Pressure groups** are groups of people who aim to influence government and public opinion over issues they feel strongly about in order to change laws or behaviour.
- Pressure groups influence companies to change by writing letters to MPs and the media, and by staging marches and publicity stunts, e.g. the Climate Group.
- The impact of pressure group activity can also influence businesses to change their marketing mix to adopt more ethical practices.
- Below are some changes made by UK supermarkets in response to pressure group activities:

  - **Products** – supermarkets have better checks in place with suppliers to ensure all meat ingredients are genuine and correctly labelled, following the horse meat scandal of 2013.
  - **Place** – sweets are no longer placed by checkout tills, as their placement was previously criticised as tempting children into pestering parents to buy them.
  - **Price** – Tesco no longer charges higher prices for 'female' coloured razors than 'male' coloured razors in a move to eliminate claims of sexist product pricing.
  - **Promotion** – supermarkets place covers over adult-aimed 'lads mags' so they are not promoted in their stores as a direct result of pressure groups complaining that such magazines can be seen by children, which is not ethical.

Quick Test

1. Define the term 'ethics'.
2. Explain how ethics can conflict with profit.
3. Give the main aim of a pressure group.

Key Words

ethics
boycott
trade-off
sustainable
pressure groups

1 Which **one** of the following is an example of an external stakeholder?
Select **one** answer. [1]

A Manager ☐

B Employee ☐

C Government ☐

D Shareholder ☐

2 Explain **one** way in which employees can impact a business. [3]

3 Explain **one** reason why it is important to update technology in a business. [3]

4 Explain **one** impact of an increase in minimum wage. [3]

5 Give **two** basic rights of an employee. [2]

6 Explain **one** impact of ensuring health and safety legislation has been met. [3]

7 Explain **one** impact on a business when consumers have higher incomes. [3]

8 a) Peter imported 1500 chairs for $20 each from the USA when the exchange rate was £1 = $1.50

Calculate how much Peter would have to pay in £.
You are advised to show your workings. [2]

b) Calculate the change in the cost for Peter in £ if the exchange rate changed to £1 = $1.80
You are advised to show your workings. [2]

9 Explain **one** way in which a decrease in interest rates might impact a business. [3]

10 Explain **one** limitation of a business using social media. [3]

11 Explain **one** benefit of digital communication. [3]

1 Which **one** of the following is an internal source of finance for a business?
Select **one** answer. [1]

A Loan capital ☐   C Retained profit ☐

B Venture capital ☐   D Stock market flotation ☐

2 Explain **one** limitation of organic growth. [3]

3 Explain **one** limitation of inorganic growth. [3]

4 Which of the following is a feature of a public limited company?
Select **one** answer. [1]

A Unlimited liability ☐   C Can sell shares on the stock market ☐

B One owner ☐   D Can lose personal possessions ☐

5 Explain **one** benefit of being a public limited company. [3]

6 Which **two** of the following are examples of organic growth?
Select **two** answers. [2]

A Merger ☐   D New market ☐

B New product ☐   E Downsizing ☐

C Takeover ☐

7   A business borrows £400 000 to fund business growth, at an interest rate of 8% for 5 years.

Calculate how much annual interest the business will pay on this loan each year.
You are advised to show your workings.   [2]

8   Explain **one** reason why a business's objectives might change over time.   [3]

9   Explain **one** impact of a decrease in the value of pound sterling (£) on a business that
exports goods and services.   [3]

10 Explain **one** limitation of a trading bloc.   [3]

11 Explain **one** possible impact on a business for being more ethical.   [3]

Product

You must be able to:

- Understand the different elements of the design mix
- Explain the phases of the product life cycle and how businesses use extension strategies
- Discuss the importance to a business of differentiating a good/service.

Design Mix

- To achieve a successful product design, a business will concentrate on three elements that make up the **design mix**: function, appearance (aesthetics) and cost.

Function

- Function is about the capabilities of the product; can it perform its intended purpose? For example, a vacuum cleaner's ability to suction dust and dirt.
- Focusing on functionality can make products unique, allowing a business to charge a higher price. This higher price allows the business to recover some of the high production costs.
- For medical equipment, functionality takes priority over cost as the equipment must perform a specific purpose.

Appearance (aesthetics)

- Aesthetics is about the look, taste or feel of a product. If the product is stylish, elegant and attractive, the chances are that it will appeal to customers and sell well.

Cost

- Businesses should produce a product as cost effectively as possible – this can lead to a competitive advantage being gained.
- High production costs lead to higher selling prices and may prevent customers buying products.
- The importance of cost is connected to the nature of the product – if a business has a focus on high quality, it will incur higher production costs.

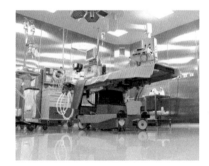

> **Key Point**
>
> The importance of the three elements of the design mix will depend on the nature of the product.

Product Life Cycle

- The **product life cycle** maps the stages a product passes through over time and the sales that can be expected from that stage.
- It can be shown in graph form and consists of the **introduction phase**, **growth phase**, **maturity phase** and **decline phase**.
- A business can map their full product range on a product life cycle graph and determine which products need more focus.

- The **introduction phase** comprises product launch.
  - Initial research, design and development will mean costs are high.
  - Sales will be low as customers are unaware that the product is for sale.
  - Businesses spend money on promotion.
  - As costs are high and sales are low, it is likely that no profit is made at this stage.
- The **growth phase** sees sales grow as awareness and popularity are increased.
  - Sales grow with demand and the business may start to make a profit.
- The **maturity phase** sees sales peak.
  - Growth of sales may slow down due to other businesses joining the market.
  - Profit may be high but start to reduce.
- The **decline phase** may see products become out-dated as tastes and technology change.
  - Sales and profits fall and a business may have to consider if it wants to continue selling the product.
- A business will try and prevent a product going into the decline phase by using extension strategies. This can be achieved by making changes to the product or promotion, lowering the price, or appealing to a new market segment.

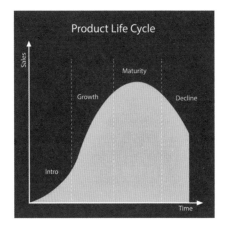

Product Differentiation

- Depending on the nature of the product, a business will choose to either focus on function, aesthetics or cost to meet their customer needs and to achieve product differentiation.
- Product differentiation can be created using the following:
  - brand image
  - unique selling point/s
  - offering a better location, features, function or design appearance
  - cheaper selling price
  - quality
  - customer service
  - product range.

Quick Test

1. Give the **three** elements of the design mix.
2. List the **two** main ways a business may extend the life cycle of its products.
3. Give **three** ways in which a business can achieve product differentiation.

Key Words

design mix
product life cycle
introduction phase
growth phase
maturity phase
decline phase
extension strategies
product differentiation

Price

You must be able to:

- Explain the different methods used by businesses to price their products
- Discuss influences on pricing strategies.

Price

- **Price** is the amount that customers pay for a product.
- Price is an important decision for businesses as price affects the amount of revenue received for each product sold.
- A business needs to carefully consider their **pricing strategy**, and this is based on a number of factors.

Pricing Strategies

- A business will decide on a price to reflect the brand and quality of its product.
- The cost of making a product will impact on the pricing. To make a profit, the price needs to be set higher than the amount it costs to make each item.
- The demand for a product will impact price as customers are willing to pay a higher price for a product that is popular.

> **Key Point**
>
> Competitors, customers and costs are considered by businesses when considering pricing strategy.

Profit Margins

- Profit margin is the difference between the sale price and the cost of production.

High margin, low volume	Low margin, high volume
A high profit margin means a business can sell fewer products (low volume) to make a profit, as the selling price is significantly higher than the cost of making the product.	A low profit margin means a business must sell a large number of products (high volume) to make a profit, as the selling price is close to the cost of making the product.

Influences on Pricing Strategies

Technology

- As e-commerce grows, customers are increasingly turning to discount and comparison websites to compare prices and seek deals. This creates a more competitive market, meaning businesses need to ensure their prices are level with competitors to appeal to customers.

- **Freemium** is a pricing strategy used mainly for digital products (such as software, media or gaming) that are offered for free. However, there is a fee (the premium) to pay if a user wants additional features, functionality or virtual goods. The digital music service Spotify is one well-known business that operates a freemium model.
- Technology has led to better machinery or tools, which means that businesses can make their goods quicker or provide a quicker service, which in turn saves costs and increases profit for the business, e.g. a taxi company uses satellite navigation that provides traffic updates and fast route options.

Competition

- Operating in a competitive environment can drive a business to reduce its pricing to remain competitive in the market.
- If a business sells a product with little differentiation, e.g. bottled water, it will have to keep prices similar to other businesses. Customers then make decisions on which products to buy based on other factors, such as quality or appearance.

Market Segments

- A business must price its products according to what customers are willing to pay. If the price is too high, the business risks making fewer sales. If it is too low, the business will not recover its costs and get into financial difficulty.

Product Life Cycle

- **Introduction and growth:** Businesses may set a low price when a product first enters the market, hoping to achieve a high volume of sales and accepting a lower profit margin. Alternatively, a business may set a high price for a new product that is innovative or has special features, often from a well-known brand. Customers may wish to be part of a premium market and the higher price increases profit.
- **Maturity:** A high price can be used to maintain profit margins. In a competitive market, a business may align prices with those of competitors to maintain its market share.
- **Decline:** A low price helps to encourage sales when customers are not prepared to pay a high amount.

> ## Quick Test
>
> 1. Give **one** pricing strategy a business may use to price its products.
> 2. Give **one** way in which technology can influence pricing strategies.
> 3. Give **one** reason why a product might be priced differently during the introduction stage compared to the decline stage of its life cycle.

Key Words
price
pricing strategy
freemium

Promotion

Quick Recall Quiz

You must be able to:

- Discuss how businesses use appropriate promotion strategies to target different market segments
- Explain how businesses use technology in promotion.

Promotion

- Promotion is about communicating to existing customers and potential customers that a product is available. It is a way of persuading customers to make a purchase.
- Promotion communicates the positioning of a product and can help to remind customers why a product is attractive to them.
- The preferences of the **market segment** are fundamental to the **promotion strategy**.
- A business will use one or a mix of these promotion strategies:
  - advertising
  - sponsorship
  - product trials
  - special offers
  - branding.

> ### Key Point
>
> Businesses need to use the appropriate promotion strategy to suit their desired market segment.

Promotion Strategies for Different Market Segments

Advertising

- A business can advertise on TV, radio, magazines and newspapers, billboards, websites, emails, through apps and many other channels.
- Advertising can target a large number of people at the same time.
- TV advertising may be more effective for the older generation.
- Younger viewers often watch TV on demand, which limits advertising, requiring businesses to advertise to this group differently (e.g. more interactive adverts on social media).

Sponsorship

- Sponsorship involves a business financially supporting or giving goods or services to an event or programme in return for advertising its brand.
- A business must use relevant events or programmes to reach its market segment and develop its brand.

Product Trials

- **Product trials** are used to get customers to try a product for the first time, usually before a business decides to launch it fully to the market.
- A large established restaurant chain may offer a new dish on its menu in restaurants in a particular area as a way of testing it.

Special Offers

- Special offers can take the form of a discount on the sales price, e.g. a complementary deal.
- A business targeted at a specific (niche) segment of the market (e.g. vegan snacks) might offer a free product if a friend is recommended.
- A business that sells products with a mass appeal (mass market), e.g. fruit juices, might offer 'buy one get one free'.

Branding

- A business can differentiate its products from those of others using an image or identity that creates a unique **brand**.
- Customers can grow loyal to a branded business and trust it.
- A branded business charges higher prices as customers are willing to pay more.

The Use of Technology in Promotion

- Targeted advertising online allows businesses to direct promotion to customers through apps, websites and social media.
- Online advertising can be targeted because browsing habits are collected through **Internet cookies** and used by businesses to tailor their advertising to Internet users. For example, if a user regularly looks at sports-related items, they will see more adverts for trainers, match tickets etc., even when they are on a website that has nothing to do with sport.
- The success of an online advertising campaign can be measured using the **click-through rate**, new followers, increased activity, or sales.
- **Viral advertising** relies on consumers passing on a promotion or advert via email or social media, which means it must grab the consumer's attention.
- **E-newsletters** are newsletters that are sent to customers via email and they can be interactive and captivating. Weblinks and QR codes allow customers to respond easily.
- Apps and social media allow customers to have a personalised user experience with the business. Businesses can easily promote their products based on the user interactions and can use influencers to help build authentic content to promote their products.

> ### Key Point
>
> Businesses can use technology to enhance their promotions through targeted advertising online, viral advertising via social media, and e-newsletters.

> ### Key Words
>
> market segment
> promotion strategy
> product trial
> brand
> Internet cookies
> click-through rate
> viral advertising
> e-newsletter

> ### Quick Test
>
> 1. Give **one** way in which a business may adapt its advertising to target younger generations.
> 2. Give **one** special offer a business could use to promote a mass market product.
> 3. Give **one** way a business can use technology to promote itself.

Place

Quick Recall Quiz

You must be able to:

- Understand the importance of place in the marketing mix
- Explain how goods and services can be distributed using retailers and e-tailers.

What is Place?

- **Place** refers to the location where customers can purchase goods and services.
- To have a successful marketing mix, a business needs to ensure their products are available in the right place at the right time for customers to purchase.
- The route that a product takes, from where it is manufactured, to where it is sold, is called the **distribution channel**.
- Most goods and services in the UK are distributed through retailers or e-tailers.

> **Key Point**
>
> In the UK, goods and services are mainly distributed through retailers and e-tailers.

Retailers

- **Retailers** are the 'middle men' – they buy large quantities of products from a **manufacturer** or a wholesaler and make the products available locally to customers.
- Retailers have a physical location for customers to visit and purchase products. This is beneficial for customers who prefer to see and try products before committing to buying them.
- Retailers can add value to their products by offering an enhanced user experience, e.g. a personal shopper service.
- As a retailer buys a large quantity of products, the price per unit will be cheaper; this reduces the profit margins for the manufacturer but allows the retailer to add their own mark-up.
- Having a physical location brings costs such as rent, fixtures and insurance.
- Retailers can take the form of: independent retailers (small shops), supermarkets, department stores, market traders, or multiples (a chain of stores).

E-tailers

- **E-tailers** are businesses that sell goods and services through the Internet.
- Some e-tailers are online-only e-tailers, such as Amazon.

- Other businesses use both e-tailing and retailing to sell their products, e.g. Argos.
- E-commerce involves electronic transactions via the Internet or electronic payment systems, e.g. contactless payments, bank cards, PayPal.
- E-tailers use e-commerce to create an online marketplace for customers and make meaningful suggestions for additional purchases. E-tailers have a global reach and allow customers the ability to shop at any time, wherever they are.
- As transactions take place over the Internet, businesses can track customers' buying habits to collect valuable market research.
- Small independent retailers or start-up businesses can benefit from using large e-tailers to distribute their products.
- E-tailers must ensure they have: user-friendly websites to attract customers; regularly updated content to meet changing customer needs; efficient **distribution** so customers can receive their orders quickly.
- It is expensive to set up e-tailing websites and customers may be reluctant to purchase over the Internet, due to fraud.

Quick Test

1. Define the term 'place'.
2. Define the terms 'retailer' and 'e-tailer'.
3. Give **three** ways in which e-tailers make purchasing goods and services more convenient for customers.

Key Words

place
distribution channel
retailer
manufacturer
e-tailer
distribution

Using the Marketing Mix to Make Business Decisions

You must be able to:

- Explain how each element of the marketing mix can influence the other elements
- Understand how businesses use the marketing mix to build a competitive advantage
- Discuss how an integrated marketing mix can influence competitive advantage.

Each Element of the Marketing Mix can Influence the Other Elements

Product

- Price – customers may demand a low-priced product so a business will need to produce their product cheaply, which will result in a lower quality product.
- Promotion – part of the promotion strategy may include changing the packaging of a product to make it more appealing to customers.
- Place – technology has led to customers changing where and when they demand their products. This has led to a change in the format of products, e.g. books are now available as e-books.

Price

- Product – strong brands and premium quality products will have higher prices.
- Promotion – special offers and discounts can reduce the price charged for a product.
- Place – an Internet-based business can charge a lower price because it doesn't have to pay costs associated with having premises.

Promotion

- Product – the life cycle of the product may influence the promotion used for it. Often when a product is new it will require lots of promotion, in contrast to the maturity stage when promotion takes place less often.
- Price – a high-priced, high-quality product will be promoted differently to a cheaper product. 'Buy one, get one free' can be used for cheaper products. Yet a high quality brand may focus on public relations.
- Place – e-tailers and high street retailers operate in a competitive environment and so offer a variety of promotions to attract customers, e.g. free delivery.

Place

- Product – cheaper goods may be sold through discount retailers.
- Price – high-priced items, such as an exclusive brand of jewellery, will be only available at exclusive stores.
- Promotion – heavy promotion will mean a product needs to be available at more locations and for an extended time, e.g. Black Friday generally means longer opening hours and a larger number of products in stock.

Marketing Mix and Competitive Advantage

- **Competitive advantage** is an advantage held by a business that allows it to perform better than its competitors.
- Innovative goods or services exceed customer needs and allow a business to gain a competitive advantage, e.g. Uber, which allows users to request cars to their exact location using an app.
- New technology or buying cheaper raw materials reduces the cost of production and allows a business to sell its products more cheaply, creating a competitive advantage.
- Effective promotion can create a competitive advantage.
- Dispatching orders quickly, offering excellent after-sales care, and being available in locations and times convenient to customers can provide great customer satisfaction, repeat purchases and possible competitive advantage.

> **Key Point**
>
> To gain a competitive advantage, a business will need to use a combination of elements in the marketing mix.

Integrated Marketing Mix Influences Competitive Advantage

- Striking the correct balance between the elements of the marketing mix is important for building a successful marketing strategy and developing a competitive advantage.
- The correct blend of product, price, promotion and place depends on: the business's objectives, the market, the size of a business, the competition, the nature of the product.

> **Quick Test**
>
> 1. Define the term 'competitive advantage'.
> 2. Explain **one** way in which the price of a product can influence promotion.
> 3. Define the term 'integrated market mix'.

> **Key Word**
>
> competitive advantage

1 Which **one** of the following is not an internal source of finance for a business? Select **one** answer. [1]

A Loan capital ☐   C Retained profit ☐

B Selling assets ☐   D Owner's savings ☐

2 Explain **one** benefit of increasing market share for a business. [3]

3 Explain **one** reason why a business may limit its own growth. [3]

4 Which of the following is **not** a feature of a public limited company? Select **one** answer. [1]

A Limited liability ☐   C Can sell shares on the stock market ☐

B One owner ☐   D Has to display its accounts to the public ☐

5 Explain **one** limitation of being a public limited company for a business. [3]

6 Which **two** of the following are examples of inorganic growth? Select **two** answers. [2]

A Merger ☐   D New market ☐

B New product ☐   E Downsizing ☐

C Takeover ☐

7 A business borrows £800 000 to fund business growth, at an interest rate of 5%.

Calculate how much annual interest the business will pay on this loan each year.
You are advised to show your workings. [2]

_____

_____

8 Explain **one** reason why a business may aim to achieve market growth. [3]

_____

_____

_____

9 Explain **one** impact of an increase in the value of pound sterling (£) on a business that imports goods and services. [3]

_____

_____

_____

10 Explain **one** benefit of a trading bloc to a business. [3]

_____

_____

_____

11 Explain **one** possible trade-off with a business being more ethical. [3]

_____

_____

_____

12 Explain **one** reason why selling assets may not be suitable to a business. [3]

_____

_____

_____

1. Which **one** of the following is an element of the design mix?
   Select **one** answer. [1]

   A Attributes ☐   C Advertising ☐

   B Accounting ☐   D Aesthetics ☐

2. Identify **two** stages of the product life cycle. [2]

3. Give **two** factors that impact on the pricing strategy of a business. [2]

4. Give **one** impact on price for a business operating in a competitive environment. [1]

5. Explain **one** advantage of 'freemium' pricing. [3]

6. Give **one** reason why a business must consider its target market when making pricing decisions. [1]

7 Define the term 'promotion'. [1]

....

....

8 Give **two** ways a business can use technology to promote its goods and services. [2]

....

....

9 Give **one** way in which place contributes to a successful marketing mix. [1]

....

....

10 Give **one** benefit of using e-newsletters. [1]

....

....

11 Explain **one** disadvantage of being an e-tailer. [3]

....

....

....

....

12 Define the term 'competitive advantage'. [1]

....

....

13 Explain **one** impact the product element of the marketing mix has on price. [3]

....

....

....

....

Business Operations

Quick Recall Quiz

You must be able to:

- State the purpose of business operations
- Identify and explain the different production processes: job, batch and flow production
- Analyse the impact of the different production processes on businesses
- Discuss the impacts of technology on production.

Production Processes

- Production is the business activity that is responsible for taking business resources and turning them into goods or services.
- As a business grows, the owners need to consider which production process is most cost effective and allows the highest level of productivity. This enables the business to price its goods and services competitively or increase its profit margins.

Job Production

- **Job production** is where one individual product is made at a time by one or a group of workers.
- Examples include a tailormade wedding dress or the HS2 (High Speed 2) rail project.

Advantages	Disadvantages
• High quality and unique products that are tailored to meet customer needs • Higher prices demanded • Workers are motivated, as they are involved in all stages of production	• Highly skilled workers required, needing training and careful management • Lengthy **production process** and higher production costs per unit

Batch Production

- **Batch production** is where similar items are grouped and made together (in batches), e.g. brown bread, white bread.
- Equipment can be easily altered to make different batches.
- Workers focus on one area of the production process.

Advantages	Disadvantages
• Variety and choice for customers • Workers become skilled in the production area, less supervision is required • More products made at once • Materials required will be purchased in bulk, so business can save on costs (economies of scale, which means the greater the quantity of materials purchased, the lower the per-unit cost, creating savings for the business)	• Demotivated workers as a result of performing the same tasks • A delay in one batch can affect the production of another batch

Flow Production

- **Flow production** is where a large number of identical products are made on an assembly line.
- Production is automated, often with extensive machinery, technology and robotics in large factories.
- Products can be made in large numbers in a short space of time.
- Examples: cars, bottled drinks.

Advantages	Disadvantages
• Raw materials are purchased in bulk, so they are cheaper, saving money for the business (economies of scale) • Goods can be produced in large quantities, so unit costs are lower • Production can be in process 24/7 without the need for breaks and holidays; quality is also improved	• Expensive to set up and buy factory, machinery and the technology required • Difficult to adapt production lines • Repetitive work leads to demotivated workers • A breakdown in one of the lines affects the entire production process

The Impacts of Technology on Production

- Lower costs – in the short term, investment is high. Machinery and factory set-up is expensive. In the long term, cost savings will come from increased productivity, lower labour costs, improved quality and less wastage.
- Increased **productivity** – machines and robots work autonomously, unlike workers who need breaks, holidays and time off.
- Improved quality – **computer aided design (CAD)** is precise, and machinery and robots reduce mistakes that can be made by human error.
- Further flexibility – **computer aided manufacture (CAM)** allows for adjustment in processes to make a variety of products, providing more flexibility for businesses and more choice for customers.

> **Key Point**
>
> Technology is changing the way in which businesses produce their products. The main impacts are to costs, productivity, quality and flexibility.

> **Key Words**
>
> job production
> production process
> batch production
> flow production
> productivity
> computer aided design (CAD)
> computer aided manufacture (CAM)

> **Quick Test**
>
> 1. Give the purpose of business operations.
> 2. Name the **three** production processes.
> 3. Name **four** impacts of technology on production.

Working with Suppliers

You must be able to:

- Interpret bar gate stock graphs and explain just in time (JIT), to understand how businesses manage stock
- Understand the factors which lead to the efficient procurement of raw materials
- Discuss the impact of logistics and supply decisions on: costs, reputation and customer satisfaction.

Stock

- **Stock** constitutes the materials a business holds for use in production or sales. Stock is also referred to as inventory.
- Stock can be: raw materials waiting to be used in the production process, stocks of materials that are not completed (work in progress) and finished goods.

> **Key Point**
>
> There is no requirement to draw a bar gate stock graph in the exam.

Bar Gate Stock Graphs

- A business can manage their stocks by setting maximum, minimum and re-order levels of stock, displayed on a **bar gate stock graph**.
- The *x*-axis on the graph shows time in weeks, the *y*-axis shows the unit of stock.
- **Maximum stock level** – the largest amount of stock that the business will hold at any one time.
- **Minimum stock level (buffer stock)** – the lowest amount of stock that a business will hold at any one time.
- The minimum stock level allows a business to continue production if delivery is delayed or if there is an unexpected increase in demand.
- **Re-order level** – the stock level where new stock will be ordered.
- **Lead time** – the time it takes for new stock to arrive once it has been ordered.
- **Order quantity** – the number of units ordered.
- The size of an order is the difference between the maximum stock level and the minimum stock level.

> **Key Point**
>
> Many businesses use specialist software to manage stock levels and automatically order stock when it reaches the reorder level.

Just In Time (JIT)

- **Just in time (JIT)** stock management is where businesses do not hold any stock; raw materials and components are ordered exactly when they are needed and used straight away in the production process.
- JIT requires regular deliveries of smaller quantities, which increases costs and requires strong supplier relationships to ensure reliability.

- Good cash-flow can be achieved as money is not tied up in stock or storage costs.
- However, economies of scale can't be utilised as raw materials are not bought in bulk.
- Supplier difficulties or a delay in delivery halts production and this can be costly for the business.

Efficient Procurement of Raw Materials

- **Procurement** is the act of obtaining or buying raw materials, components or services from a supplier to be used in the production of goods and services.
- Businesses need to maintain a good relationship with their suppliers. When choosing a supplier, a business will need to consider the following factors:
  - **quality** – suppliers need to provide a business with the best quality raw materials or services for the best price.
  - **delivery** – suppliers should be reliable, deliver on time, at short notice and with reasonable delivery costs
  - **availability** – suppliers need to have stock or components available when a business orders
  - **cost** – a business will want raw materials cheaply and the option to pay by trade credit.
  - **trust** – suppliers want to be treated fairly and paid on time. Honest communication and joint problem solving will develop the trust between a supplier and a business.

The Impact of Logistics and Supply Decisions

- A business needs to ensure careful planning goes into decisions about their **logistics** and suppliers.
- A reliable supplier may be more expensive and increase costs for a business. However, the business can rest assured that the supplier will be able to meet demand and produce good quality products for its customers. This ensures customer satisfaction and a good reputation for the business and its brand.
- Distance between factories and a supplier needs careful planning – being in close proximity to suppliers means delivery times are not too long and allows for flexibility should unexpected orders need to be made.

Key Words

stock
bar gate stock graph
maximum stock level
minimum stock level
  (buffer stock)
re-order level
lead time
order quantity
just in time (JIT)
procurement
logistics

> **Quick Test**
>
> 1. Give the elements shown on a bar gate stock graph.
> 2. Define 'just in time' stock control.
> 3. Give the **five** factors that a business should consider when choosing a supplier.

Managing Quality

You must be able to:

- Define quality
- Explain the difference between quality control and quality assurance
- Discuss the importance of managing quality in allowing a business to control costs and gain a competitive advantage.

Quality

- **Quality** is about meeting a minimum set of standards to satisfy customer expectations for a good or service.
- High quality can be achieved by using quality raw materials, a quality design process, quality packaging and branding, durability and good customer service.
- Quality should be customer driven and if a business can build a reputation for high quality, it can develop a competitive advantage.
- Many customers rely on reviews from social media and review websites before deciding to purchase a good or service. If a business has a reputation for good quality, customers will choose them over competitors and be willing to pay higher prices.
- Good quality can be achieved through **quality control** or **quality assurance**.

The Difference between Quality Control and Quality Assurance

Quality Control

- Quality control is where finished products are inspected to see if they meet minimum standards. This approach checks for product defects rather than preventing defects from occurring.
- Quality standards are achieved before products reach customers; if a product is found to have a defect it is rectified or sold as a sub-standard product. This approach is costly as it could result in a large amount of wastage because the end of the production process is too late to test for quality, and quality is checked by inspectors and not by workers.

Quality Assurance

- Quality assurance is where quality is part of the production process; quality is checked at every stage by workers.
- Every worker takes responsibility for quality; although time consuming, this approach should result in zero defect production. Workers tend to be motivated by having more involvement in the production process and being part of a business where quality is primary.

- Quality inspectors are not required but management must train workers effectively and set up adequate systems to test quality and reduce inconsistencies.
- Customers' needs are prioritised in the production process and businesses can assure customers that products are good quality.

The Importance of Managing Quality

- If a business has effective quality management systems, it will experience less wastage in defective products and the cost of production will be reduced.
- If the cost of production is lower, profit margins increase.
- Good quality products meet customers' needs. This is a method of adding value, allowing businesses to charge higher prices and grow their market share.
- Building quality management into the production process can be expensive. A business will weigh this up against the potential increased sales from customers and brand reputation for good quality.
- A business will need to invest the time in finding out customer expectations as they differ based on the business, e.g. customers have different expectations from a budget airline and a premium airline.
- To gain a competitive advantage, a business needs to offer better quality goods or services than competitors at a competitive price.

Budget airline

Premium airline

Key Words

quality
quality control
quality assurance

The Sales Process

You must be able to:

- Discuss the factors that contribute to an effective sales process
- Analyse the importance to a business of providing good customer service.

The Sales Process

- The **sales process** is a circular process; if a customer is satisfied with their sales experience, they should return to repeat purchase, and may do so time and time again.
- The five key stages of the sales process are:
  - product knowledge
  - speed and efficiency of service
  - customer engagement
  - customer feedback
  - post-sales service.
- **Product knowledge** is important for a sales person as it enables the features and benefits of products to be effectively communicated to customers.
- Sales people should have the ability to match a customer's needs to suitable products on offer by the business; the customer can then make an informed choice.
- **Speed and efficiency of service** are fundamental to ensuring customer needs are met; customers should be served in a timely manner and be provided with the correct items that have been requested.
- Customers may have different standards, dependent on the nature of the business, e.g. a fast food restaurant is expected to serve customers quickly, but in a restaurant a longer wait is expected.
- **Customer engagement** is concerned with the experiences of customers with a business or brand and the connection that is built through nurturing and managing this relationship.
- Customer engagement can be achieved through various channels of correspondence, both offline and online.
- If a business can keep customers engaged, their interest can turn into sales.
- A response to customer feedback is required to maintain good relationships with customers.
- A business needs to ensure that positive and negative **customer feedback** is acted on as this is effective market research.
- If a customer is unhappy with a business or leaves a bad review, this must be handled in a sensitive way to try and resolve the situation and to keep the customer's business.

> ### Key Point
>
> The important aspects of the sales process include: product knowledge, efficiency of service, customer engagement, customer feedback and post-sales service.

- **Post-sales service** is concerned with the procedures that a business has in place to support customers after the sale of a good or service. Examples include warranty or repair services.

Customer Service

Good Customer Service

- Good customer service has many benefits for a business.
- Happy customers feel valued, are loyal and will repeat purchase.
- If customers are loyal to a business, it is much harder for competitors to get them to try their products.
- Satisfied customers tell others about their good experiences and this could attract more people to the business.
- Satisfied customers can help create a positive working environment and make a business a reputable employer.
- A business can gain a reputation for good customer service and this can develop into a competitive advantage.

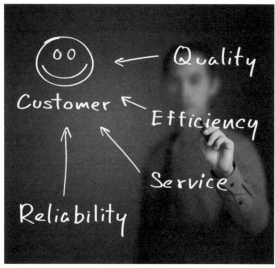

Bad Customer Service

- Poor customer service will lead to complaints and a loss of sales for a business.
- Bad customer service can have a negative impact on the reputation of a business as customers may share their negative experiences with family and friends or post bad reviews online for new potential customers to see.
- Bad reviews can have a negative impact on overall sales for a business, lowering revenue and profit.
- A loss of reputation can contribute to a business losing its position in the market, or can leave it vulnerable to being taken over by competitors.

> **Quick Test**
>
> 1. Give the **five** factors that are important in the sales process.
> 2. Give **one** benefit of offering good customer service.
> 3. Explain **one** way in which poor customer service can impact a business.

> **Key Words**
>
> sales process
> customer engagement
> post-sales service

1 Define the term 'function'. [1]

2 Give **one** purpose of using an extension strategy. [1]

3 Discuss **one** reason why businesses may not be profitable during the introduction stage of the product life cycle. [6]

4 Which **two** of the following are examples of promotion strategies?
Select **two** answers. [2]

A Special offers ☐

B Product trials ☐

C Price ☐

D Product ☐

E Refunds ☐

5 Give **one** advantage of using targeted advertising online. [1]

6 Define the term 'distribution channel'. [1]

7 Give **one** example of how retailers add value to products. [1]

8 Explain **one** advantage of being an e-tailer. [3]

9 Give **two** factors that influence a business achieving an integrated marketing mix. [2]

1. Give **one** advantage of the job production process. [1]

2. Explain **one** disadvantage of flow production. [3]

3. Explain **one** way in which technology has increased productivity for businesses. [3]

4. Give **two** examples of stock a business may hold. [2]

5. Define the term 'minimum stock level' (or 'buffer stock'). [1]

6. Explain **one** reason why supplier relationships are important if a business operates just in time stock control. [3]

7 Give **one** reason why quality management systems reduce the cost of production. [1]

8 Explain **one** impact of effective staff training as part of the quality assurance approach. [3]

9 Give **one** way a business can use the sales process to collect market research data. [1]

10 Define the term 'post-sales service'. [1]

11 Give **one** impact of bad customer service. [1]

Business Calculations

Quick Recall Quiz

You must be able to:

- Understand the concept and calculation of gross profit and net profit
- Calculate and interpret gross profit margin, net profit margin and average rate of return.

Sales Revenue

- **Sales revenue** is:
  - how much a business receives in payment from selling goods and services
  - also called 'income', 'revenue' or 'turnover'.
- A business needs to know how much revenue it has received to be able to calculate profit (once costs are deducted).
- The formula for sales revenue is: selling price × quantity sold.

Costs

- **Costs** are the operating expenses a business must pay.
- A business needs to know how much its costs are to be able to calculate profit (after deducting costs from sales revenue).
- Different types of costs: **fixed costs**, **variable costs** and **total costs**.

Fixed costs
• Stay the same regardless of output
• Are **indirect costs** (not directly linked with the production of the goods or service being produced and sold)
• Remain the same regardless of how many goods or services are made and sold
• Examples include rent, advertising and manager salaries

Variable costs
• Change directly with the level of output
• Are usually **direct costs**, which are directly linked with the production of goods or services
• The more goods or services made and sold, the higher the variable costs will be
• Are also known as **cost of goods sold**
• Examples include raw materials, raw ingredients, packaging, overtime wages and wages of temporary staff

Total costs
• Are calculated by adding all fixed costs and variable costs together

What is Profit?

- **Profit** is the difference between how much revenue a business receives and how much it has to pay out in costs.
- Profit is difficult to make in the first year or two of operation; so a **loss** is often made by new businesses.
- **Gross profit** is the calculation of how much profit a business makes from selling goods or services after it has deducted the cost of sales (costs incurred directly).

- The formula for gross profit is: sales revenue – cost of sales.
- Gross profit should be expressed in units of currency, e.g. £.
- **Net profit** is found after the deduction of other operating expenses (such as fixed costs) and bank interest.
  - The formula for net profit is: gross profit – other operating expenses and interest.
  - Net profit should be expressed in units of currency, e.g. £.

Profit/Profitability
- Profit and **profitability** are not the same thing.
- Profit is how much profit has been made.
- Profitability looks at how good a business is at making a profit.

Profitability Ratios
- Profitability ratios help a business:
  - calculate its ability to make profit
  - measure how effectively the business converts revenues into profit
  - measure whether the profit is enough to finance reinvestment
  - measure how well the business compares with the rest of the industry it operates in.
- **Gross profit margin** is: gross profit ÷ sales revenue × 100. The answer should be expressed as a percentage (%).
- Gross profit margin shows how efficient a business is in converting the cost of sales bought into profit.
- The lower the gross profit margin, the more stock a business has to sell to make a sustainable profit.
- **Net profit margin** is: net profit ÷ sales revenue × 100.
  - When this formula is used, the answer is expressed as a percentage (%).
- Net profit margin shows how profitable a business is when all costs are taken into account.
- If the net profit margin is considerably lower than the gross profit margin, it suggests that overheads are high and should be reduced.
- The **average rate of return (ARR)** is: average annual profit (total profit ÷ number of years) ÷ cost of investment × 100.
  - When this formula is used, the answer should be expressed as a percentage (%).
- ARR calculates how much an entrepreneur or investor is getting back on the money invested and can be compared to bank interest rates.
- ARR does not take cash-flow into account.

See page 139 for formulae used in business calculations.

See page 139 for formulae used in business calculations.

> **Quick Test**
>
> 1. Define the terms 'gross profit' and 'net profit'.
> 2. Define the terms 'profit' and 'profitability'.
> 3. Define the term 'average rate of return'.

Revise

Key Point

Gross profit looks at how much profit a business has made on the revenue it has received once the cost of sales has been deducted. Net profit looks at how much profit has been made after all costs have been deducted.

Key Words

sales revenue
costs
fixed costs
variable costs
total costs
indirect costs
direct costs
cost of goods sold
profit
loss
gross profit
net profit
profitability
gross profit margin
net profit margin
average rate of return (ARR)

Understanding Business Performance

You must be able to:

- Use and interpret quantitative business data to support, inform and justify business decisions
- Analyse the use and limitations of financial information in business performance and decision making.

What is Quantitative Business Data?

- **Quantitative business data** is numerical and statistical data.
- Businesses use graphs and charts to present a lot of quantitative data in one place.
- Graphs, tables and charts are a visual and easy way of expressing information and can often show trends and other important considerations.
- Sometimes businesses share quantitative data in the form of numbers, such as percentages, which show accuracy and allow for comparisons with historic figures, other businesses and the industry standard.
- Quantitative business data can be collected from primary or secondary sources:
  - primary data is collected first-hand by someone for a specific reason
  - secondary data relates to information that is second-hand.

> **Key Point**
>
> Quantitative data is useful, however it needs to be accurate and interpreted correctly to be of proper use, especially if it is being used to make commercial decisions.

What is Financial Data?

- **Financial data** refers to past, present and future records of the financial health of a business, e.g. financial and accounting records, sales, marketing and salary data.
- Sharing of some financial data is mandatory, while some can remain private.
- Sole traders and partnerships have to share financial records of their income, expenses, VAT records (if they are over the VAT threshold) and Pay As You Earn (PAYE) records (if they hire staff).
- Sole traders have to keep bank statements as proof. However, this data is not shared with the public.
- Companies have to provide copies of their accounts every year and file them with Companies House. These accounts include a balance sheet (statement of financial position) and a statement of profit and loss (statement of comprehensive income), which are available for the public to view.
- Unlike sole traders and partnerships, companies must also pay auditors to prepare their accounts for them.

How can Financial Data be Used?

- Financial data can be used to:
  - show trends within a business
  - apply to a bank for a loan
  - apply to investors for investment analysis.

What is Marketing Data?

- **Marketing data** is data that helps a business make decisions.
- It may be data that a business has collected themselves (primary data), e.g. from a questionnaire about customer preferences, or it could be data that already exists (secondary data), which the business finds useful.
- Marketing data has information about sales forecasts, promotional plans and customer preferences.

What is Market Data?

- **Market data** refers to information that relates to a variety of investment markets, including:
  - live prices of stocks and shares on the stock exchange market
  - exchange rates on the currency markets that show the latest buying and selling rates for different currencies
  - **commodities** on the commodity market that show the price of many of life's necessities, which can affect everyone, e.g. oil.

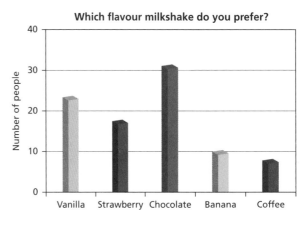

Which flavour milkshake do you prefer?

The Use and Limitations of Financial Information

- Many stakeholders use financial information to interpret past business performance.
- This can show if a business has been successful.
- Limitations of financial information include:
  - it may only be a snapshot of a certain period of time
  - it can quickly become out of date
  - it may be inaccurate as the data collected may be biased or might have missed out vital contributing factors
  - two people reading the same quantitative data may have different ways of understanding it.

Quick Test

1. Define the term 'quantitative data'.
2. Define the terms 'marketing Data' and 'market data'.
3. List **three** limitations of using financial information.

Key Words

quantitative business data
financial data
marketing data
market data
commodities

1 Give **two** production processes. [2]

2 Explain **one** advantage of the batch production process. [3]

3 Explain **one** advantage that a reliable supplier brings to a business. [3]

4 Define the term 'procurement'. [1]

5 Identify **two** costs associated with holding large quantities of stock. [2]

6 Explain **one** advantage of quality assurance to a business. [3]

7 Explain **one** advantage of producing good quality products. [3]

_____

_____

_____

_____

8 Give **one** reason why product knowledge is important in the sales process. [1]

_____

_____

9 Explain **one** factor that a business should consider when choosing between suppliers. [3]

_____

_____

_____

_____

1 Explain **one** way a business can increase its gross profit. [3]

....

....

....

2 Give **two** examples of a fixed cost. [2]

....

....

3 The table below shows the financial records of a business.

Total revenue	£18 000
Cost of sales	£10 000
Gross profit	£8000
Overheads	£5000

a) Using the information above, calculate the net profit of the business.
   You are advised to show your workings. [2]

....

....

b) Using the information above, calculate the gross profit margin of the business.
   You are advised to show your workings. [2]

....

....

4 Explain **one** way in which the net profit margin of a business might decrease. [3]

....

....

....

5 The table below shows the financial records of a business.

Total revenue	£45 000
Cost of sales	
Gross profit	£15 000
Overheads	£10 000
Net profit	

Using the information above, calculate the cost of sales and net profit of the business.
You are advised to show your workings. [2]

6 The table below shows information about a business.

Sales revenue	£50 000
Gross profit	£20 000
Expenses	£10 000

a) Using the information above, calculate the gross profit margin of the business.
You are advised to show your workings. [2]

b) Using the information above, calculate the net profit margin.
You are advised to show your workings. [2]

7 The table below shows information about a business.

Average annual profit	£5000
Initial investment	£40 000

Using the information above, calculate the average rate of return for this investment. [2]

Organisational Structures

You must be able to:

- Explain different organisational structures and when each are appropriate
- Assess different ways of working
- Analyse the importance of effective communication.

Organisational Structures

- **Organisational structures** are:
  - charts that look similar to family trees – they can be **hierarchical** (also known as tall) or **flat**
  - useful for showing the internal structure and the roles and responsibilities of staff in businesses.

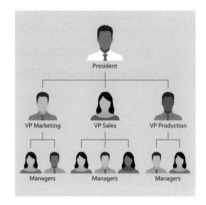

Hierarchical Structures

- Have lots of levels of authority.
- Can motivate staff to strive for the next level of promotion due to their many management levels.
- Can be expensive (lots of managerial salaries).
- Communication can be slow and distorted due to numerous levels of authority.
- Examples: NHS, local government, the police force.

Flat Structures

- Have few levels of authority.
- Are responsive to change (staff have the **autonomy** (authority) to make decisions).
- May leave staff feeling overwhelmed if there are few levels of management for support.
- Examples: small family businesses, the creative industries.

Business Decisions

- Some businesses prefer big decisions to be made by senior management in a head office; this is known as being **centralised**.
- With centralisation, all branches or stores of a business will have the same policies, prices and look.
- Centralisation can slow communication between the shopfloor and senior management – to overcome this, some businesses prefer to be **decentralised**.
- Decentralised businesses make decisions at a local level, by local managers who know what their customers' needs are and can quickly respond to them without having to refer to Head Office.

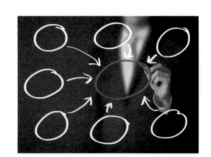

Effective Communication

- It is vital for a business to have strong communication with all of its managers, staff and customers; this minimises mistakes.
- A business with too little communication can leave staff feeling ignored and stressed; without specific communication, staff may make wrong decisions – causing mistakes, wastage, loss of time and poor **motivation** levels – which can decrease productivity.
- A business with too much communication can give staff too much information; staff might feel overwhelmed by emails or by attending too many meetings.
- Sometimes communication is poor due to other reasons, such as:
  - it uses too much **jargon**
  - it uses the wrong language, which is open to misinterpretation
  - it may be biased or untruthful
  - it may not seek feedback (or act upon feedback) from staff or customers.

Key Point

Too much communication is just as risky as too little communication.

Different Ways of Working

- **Full-time** staff work for around 35 hours per week (and, due to regulation, no more than 48 hours per week).
- **Part-time** staff gain the same benefits as full-time staff but work for less than 35 hours a week.
- Working hours can be rigid, e.g. 9–5, or flexible.
- **Flexible hours** are when someone will work the number of hours they are contracted to but with more choice over when they work.
- Contracts may be **permanent** (on an 'until-further-notice basis') or **temporary**.
- Businesses may have staff they permanently hire (on a full-time, part-time or flexi-time basis) for day-to-day work and recruit temporary staff for busy periods or to cover staff holiday or sickness (on a temporary basis).
- **Freelance contracts** are when someone is self-employed and they choose to work for different businesses on a contract-by-contract basis.
- Freelance workers tend to be highly specialist, e.g. architects.
- Technology has brought change to the work environment; people are able to work together from different locations, which is known as **remote working**.

Key Words

organisational structure
hierarchical
flat
autonomy
centralised
decentralised
motivation
jargon
full-time
part-time
flexible hours
permanent contracts
temporary contracts
freelance contracts
remote working

Quick Test

1. Define the term 'organisational structure'.
2. Define the terms 'centralised' and 'decentralised' structures.
3. Define the term 'remote working'.

Effective Recruitment

Quick Recall Quiz

You must be able to:

- Explain different job roles and responsibilities
- Explain how businesses recruit people and the documents required to do this
- Analyse the usefulness of internal and external recruitment.

Key Job Roles

- Sole traders and partnerships are the main decision makers for their business, however they may want or need to employ staff to work with them.
- Private limited companies and public limited companies have boards of **directors** who are the people responsible for the business. Directors:
  - meet regularly to decide the aims and objectives of the business
  - make decisions that affect all the stakeholders, not just the company's shareholders
  - are the people who decide whether dividends will be paid (paying profits to shareholders)
  - need to be aware of their legal responsibilities as directors
  - may decide to employ **senior managers** to be responsible for the day-to-day operations of the business in order for aims and objectives to be achieved.
- Senior managers might need to hire **supervisors** or **team leaders** to help them communicate with, manage and motivate staff.
- Supervisors and team leaders work with staff and have the authority to delegate work, reward and discipline staff; as **line managers**, they are in charge of staff during their shift and are normally paid a higher salary for this responsibility.
- **Operational staff** are staff hired to look after other day-to-day jobs, such as receptionists and administration staff.
- **Support staff** are those who carry out specific jobs that facilitate business success, e.g. (IT) technicians, canteen staff.

Internal Recruitment

- **Internal recruitment** is when a business appoints someone for a job who already works for the business. With internal recruitment:
  - the member of staff is familiar with the business and the business knows that the applicant is reliable
  - there is no need for expensive advertising and induction training
  - if a member of staff moves from one role to another within the business, their old job still needs to be filled

- some members of staff may be resentful if a colleague is promoted for a job they desire
- methods of advertising include: notices in staff rooms, emails, management recommendation and announcements at meetings.

External Recruitment

- **External recruitment** is when people are hired from outside of the business. With external recruitment:
  - new recruits are often highly motivated, highly productive and bring new ideas
  - new recruits will require expensive induction training and time to settle into the role; they may also need support from other staff, which might slow existing staff productivity
  - advertising for external recruitment can be an expensive and lengthy process, e.g. senior members of staff might have to **give notice** of three months with their existing employer
  - methods of advertising include: online advertising, notices in Job Centres, recruitment agencies, advertising in newspapers.

Documentation for Recruitment

- A **CV** (curriculum vitae) is a summary of personal, career, education and skills details.
- An applicant may leave their CV with a business to consider.
- A **job description** is a document prepared by a business that explains the responsibilities and duties of a job.
- A **person specification** is a document prepared by a business that explains what it is seeking in any applicant for a job; the specification lists essential and desirable qualifications, skills, attitudes, characteristics and experience.
- A **job application form** is a form prepared by a business for a candidate to complete when applying for a job. An application form allows specific questions to be asked, in a standardised format that helps a business to treat all staff equally.

Hiring process

Job Posting > Review of Applications > In-Person Interview > Job Testing > Job Offer

> ## Quick Test
>
> 1. List the levels in a hierarchical structure.
> 2. Give **two** benefits of external recruitment.
> 3. List the **four** main documents required for the recruitment process.

Key Point

A job description is information about the duties and responsibilities of the job. A person specification explains what skills, experience, qualifications, attitude and qualities an applicant will need to possess to do the job.

Key Words

directors
senior managers
supervisors/team leaders
line managers
operational staff
support staff
internal recruitment
external recruitment
give notice
CV
job description
person specification
job application form

Effective Training and Development

You must be able to:

- Explain how businesses train and develop employees
- Explain why businesses train and develop employees
- Analyse the benefits of training and development to a business.

What is Training and Development?

- Training is the action of teaching a person new skills.
- Development is improving or perfecting existing skills.

Types of Training

Formal Training

- Formal training is when a business arranges for staff to have training that has specific objectives. Formal training:
  - is provided by specialists and tends to be away from work, e.g. when employees go on a course to gain a new qualification with other learners from different businesses
  - is highly structured; upon completion the employee may be given a certificate
  - is of a high standard; it allows employees to learn without interruptions
  - is expensive and takes a member of staff away from the workplace.

Informal Training

- Informal training is when a business arranges for staff to receive less structured training. Informal training:
  - usually takes place within the workplace and involves other team members to provide training
  - is useful for teaching staff how to use specific equipment, e.g. how to use a till
  - can be tailored to the employee in a familiar setting
  - is quick and cheap to arrange
  - is sometimes not taken seriously and relies on the expertise of the trainer.

Self-learning

- Self-learning is when an employee studies without the presence of a teacher or colleague. Self-learning:
  - often includes computer courses, online learning and watching videos
  - allows employees to learn at their own pace
  - is cheap
  - does not allow the learner to get immediate feedback or questions answered because there is no teacher.

Observation

- **Observation** (often called 'shadowing') is when an employee watches another member of staff to learn how a job is done. With observation:
  - staff are able to ask questions
  - the member of staff being observed is able to check understanding by asking questions
  - sometimes members of staff do not enjoy being observed, which can cause resentment
  - the training is only as good as the member of staff being observed; they may teach bad habits.

Training and Business Target Setting

- Successful businesses tend to regularly review their aims and objectives.
- This involves constantly reviewing legal, marketing, customer needs and technological changes; this can help with target setting.
- Staff need to be trained to keep up with all of these changes through **ongoing training**.
- Through regular **appraisals** with staff, businesses can identify gaps in knowledge or skills and devise a training plan by setting targets for individuals, monitoring their progress through **performance reviews**.
- Performance reviews are formal and give staff feedback on their performance over a period of time.

Why Businesses Train and Develop Staff

- Businesses need to train staff to be able to carry out their roles effectively.
- Staff who are better trained:
  - are more likely to produce better quality goods and services, which means less wastage and more efficiency, which reduces costs
  - can be more productive, which can benefit the business and help them produce more
  - often have higher levels of motivation and are more likely to enjoy their roles, giving better customer service
  - can help to attract new recruits to the business who are interested in career development.
- The benefits arising from better trained staff help to create a competitive advantage for the business.

Key Point

Training and developing staff can be expensive but if done effectively can help staff keep up to date with changes in technology, bringing business efficiency and competitiveness. Staff training and development also improves productivity, quality and staff motivation.

Key Words

training
development
formal training
informal training
self-learning
observation
ongoing training
appraisals
performance reviews

Quick Test

1. Define the term 'formal training'.
2. Define the term 'self-learning'.
3. Explain **one** benefit to a business of staff training.

Motivation

You must be able to:

* Explain the importance of motivation in the workplace
* Explain how businesses motivate employees
* Analyse the importance of having a highly motivated workforce.

Benefits of a Motivated Workforce

* Motivation is about encouraging staff to want to give their best effort and care about the business they work for.
  A motivated workforce:
  - is more likely to attract new recruits because if applicants see that people are enjoying their work, they are more likely to want to work for the business; the more applicants a business has, the larger the talent pool it can choose from, which means it should be able to hire the best quality staff
  - is more likely to recommend others to come and work for the business, which can save on job advertising costs
  - is more likely to lead to lower absenteeism
  - can reduce **staff turnover**, which is the percentage of staff who leave a business during a certain period of time
  - is more likely to bring new ideas to a business because the staff care about its success
  - is more likely to give better customer service because staff satisfaction shows
  - is more likely to be productive and efficient, which can increase quality output and reduce mistakes, thus increasing profit.

Financial Methods of Motivation

* **Remuneration** means financial payment for work completed or services performed.
* Some people are motivated by high remuneration and work harder if they know they will be paid more.
* Workers on a **piece rate** (which is a method of paying staff according to how many pieces of work they produce) may be motivated to work more quickly to produce more goods or services if they know their **wages** will be higher, however a business will need to make sure that quality does not suffer if workers rush their jobs.
* Some businesses pay staff a **bonus** if they achieve performance review targets.
* Bonuses can be an incentive for staff to try their hardest to achieve a relatively hard target, which is a motivator for people who like a challenge.

- However, businesses have to be careful their staff do not cut corners to reach these targets. Also, after the target is reached, some staff stop giving their best effort because they have already been rewarded.
- **Commission** is a method used to pay staff once they have either made or sold something.
- With commission, the employee tends not to receive payment until they have made or sold a particular thing, e.g. an estate agent will be paid once a house has been sold.
- **Fringe benefits** (perks) are when a business rewards its staff with something of financial value, such as free gym membership.
- Fringe benefits are not always taxed, or are taxed at a lower rate, so the employee benefits from a higher net income.
- Some staff are interested in fringe benefits because they can save them a lot of money in expensive life luxuries.
- **Promotion** is another financial motivator; if staff know there is the possibility of promotion to a higher level of work, they may be more likely to perform to their best ability.

Non-financial Methods of Motivation

- **Job enrichment** is when a business tries to make a job more demanding and less boring in order to motivate staff.
- Some low skilled, boring jobs can benefit from **job rotation**, which means that staff are given short periods of time on various other tasks within the business.
- Praising staff is sometimes the most effective method of motivation.
- **Autonomy** involves giving staff responsibility to manage their own work; this allows staff to feel trusted, which can be motivating.

 Key Point

A business can provide financial rewards or non-financial rewards to motivate staff.

 Key Words

staff turnover
remuneration
piece rate
wages
bonus
commission
fringe benefits
promotion
job enrichment
job rotation

Quick Test

1. Define the term 'motivation'.
2. List **three** benefits to a business of having a motivated workforce.
3. Define the term 'fringe benefit'.

1 Explain **one** limitation of financial data. [3]

2 Explain **one** benefit of using average rate of return. [3]

3 The table below shows information about a business.

Sales revenue	£100 000
Gross profit	£70 000
Net profit	£30 000

a) Using the information above, calculate the cost of sales and overheads for the business.
You are advised to show your workings. [2]

b) Using the information above, calculate the gross profit margin.
You are advised to show your workings. [2]

c) Using the information above, calculate the net profit margin.
You are advised to show your workings. [2]

4 The table below shows information about a business.

Total profit	£100 000
Number of years	5
Initial investment	£200 000

Using the information above, calculate the average rate of return for this investment. [2]

5 Give **one** reason why a business may use profitability ratios. [1]

6 A business sells its products for £5 each. The fixed costs the business has to pay each month are £25 000 and the variable cost is £2.50 per product.

Calculate the net profit for the business if it sells 50 000 units each month.
You are advised to show your workings. [2]

7 The table below shows the financial records of a business.

Total revenue	
Cost of sales	£80 000
Gross profit	£150 000
Overheads	
Net profit	£100 000

Using the information above, calculate the total revenue and overheads of the business.
You are advised to show your workings. [2]

1 Explain **one** benefit of a centralised organisational structure.   [3]

2 Explain **one** impact of appointing temporary staff.   [3]

3 Explain **one** benefit of a decentralised organisational structure.   [3]

4 Which **one** of the following describes when decision making is passed down the hierarchy?
   Select **one** answer.   [1]

   A Decentralised ☐   **C** Flat ☐

   B Centralised ☐   **D** Tall ☐

5 Explain **one** impact of remote working on a business.   [3]

6 Which **one** of the following is a document used when applying for a job?
   Select **one** answer.   [1]

   A CV ☐   **C** Person specification ☐

   B Job description ☐   **D** Job advert ☐

7 Which **one** of the following is a document that informs a job applicant of the skills and qualifications required?
Select **one** answer.   [1]

A CV ☐   **C** Person specification ☐

B Job description ☐   **D** Job advert ☐

8 Explain **one** limitation of internal recruitment.   [3]

9 Explain **one** limitation of external recruitment.   [3]

10 Explain **one** financial method of increasing employee motivation.   [3]

11 Which **one** of the following is a benefit of training employees?
Select **one** answer.   [1]

A Increased productivity ☐   **C** Increased labour turnover ☐

B Decreased motivation ☐   **D** Increased absenteeism ☐

12 Explain **one** non-financial method of increasing employee motivation.   [3]

1 Explain **one** purpose of a person specification. [3]

2 Explain **one** barrier to effective communication. [3]

3 Explain **one** benefit of a motivated workforce. [3]

4 Which **one** of the following is likely to decrease as a result of training employees?
Select **one** answer. [1]

A Labour turnover ☐   C Efficiency ☐

B Productivity ☐   D Motivation ☐

5 Explain **one** limitation of formal training. [3]

6 Explain **one** limitation of a centralised organisational structure. [3]

7 Explain **one** limitation of a decentralised organisational structure. [3]

....

....

....

8 Explain **one** reason for the importance of training staff with new technology. [3]

....

....

....

9 Which **one** of the following is the document that explains the roles and requirements of a new job role?

Select **one** answer. [1]

A Person specification ☐ **C** Job description ☐

B Job advert ☐ **D** CV ☐

10 Which **one** of the following is a standardised document that candidates fill out when applying for a job?

Select **one** answer. [1]

A Person specification ☐ **C** Application form ☐

B Job advert ☐ **D** CV ☐

11 Explain **one** limitation of financial methods of motivation. [3]

....

....

....

12 Identify **one** limitation of non-financial methods of motivation. [1]

....

....

Mixed Questions

1 Explain **one** benefit of using 'just in time' production. [3]

2 Explain **one** appropriate objective for an established business. [3]

3 Explain **one** impact to a business if the unemployment rate decreases. [3]

4 Explain **one** benefit of using retained profit as a source of finance. [3]

5 Explain **one** limitation of quantitative data. [3]

6   Explain **one** purpose of calculating the break-even point.   [3]

7   Explain **one** purpose of a market map.   [3]

8   Explain **one** benefit of good communication.   [3]

9   Explain **one** limitation of quality assurance.   [3]

10   Explain **one** reason why a business keeps financial records.   [3]

11   Explain **one** limitation of a tall organisational structure.   [3]

Mixed Questions

12 Explain **one** benefit of quality assurance. [3]

13 Explain **one** potential conflict between two different types of stakeholders. [3]

14 Explain **one** purpose of a tariff. [3]

15 Explain **one** way in which high inflation might affect a business. [3]

16 Explain **one** way in which e-commerce can reduce the costs of a business. [3]

17 Explain **one** reason why it is important for a business to differentiate its products. [3]

18 The table below shows information about a business.

Inflow	£20 000
Outflow	£12 000
Opening balance	£4 000

Using the information above, calculate the closing balance for the business. [2]

19 Explain **one** risk of running a business. [3]

20 Explain **one** reason why income might impact the price a business might set. [3]

21 Which **one** of the following is the formula for gross profit?
Select **one** answer. [1]

A   cost of sales – total revenue   ☐

B   cost of sales + total revenue   ☐

C $\dfrac{\text{total revenue}}{\text{cost of sales}} \times 100$ ☐

D   total revenue – cost of sales   ☐

22 Explain **one** advantage of being part of a trading bloc to a business. [3]

Mixed Questions

23 Which **one** of the following is **not** an element of the marketing mix?
Select **one** answer. [1]

A Product ☐

B Promotion ☐

C Production ☐

D Price ☐

24 Explain **one** reason why it is important for a business to retain employees. [3]

25 Explain **one** reason why a business might recruit a freelance worker. [3]

26 Explain **one** reason why a business will have buffer stock levels. [3]

27 Explain **one** reason why a business may choose to become more ethical. [3]

28 Explain **one** reason why a business may choose to relocate its production abroad.   [3]

29 Explain **one** impact an increase in legislation might have on a business.   [3]

30 Explain **one** purpose of a business plan.   [1]

31 Which **one** of the following is the formula for total cost?
Select **one** answer.   [1]

   A fixed cost – variable cost ☐

   B fixed cost + total cost ☐

   C fixed cost + variable cost ☐

   D total cost – variable cost ☐

Answers

Pages 6–7

1. Can adapt goods and services to meet changing customer needs, which will give the business a unique selling point and therefore a reason for customers to continue to purchase its product.
2. Changes in technology; Changes in consumers' tastes; Goods and services becoming outdated/obsolete.
3. No longer produced or used; outdated

Pages 8–9

1. Business failure; Loss of money; Lack of a secure income.
2. Careful planning and market research.
3. The owner having independence and making their own business decisions.

Pages 10–11

1. A physical product that can be touched.
2. **Any one from:** produce goods and services; meet customer needs; add value.
3. capital; land; labour

1. **Possible answer:** To survive [1] and grow [1] and continue to meet the changing needs of customers [1].
2. **Any one from:** first to meet customer needs for that product [1]; gains a competitive advantage [1].
3. C [1]
4. **Any one from:** The demand for products can change [1]; The business may need to adapt its product [1].
5. The things that may go wrong when setting up a business [1].
6. **Possible answer:** Being in full control as the boss [1], making all the business decisions [1] and deciding when and what times to work [1].
7. **Possible answer:** Not having financial security as entrepreneurs give up previous employment [1] and do not have a guaranteed regular income [1]. There is a risk that financial commitments cannot be met if the business isn't successful [1].
8. C [1]
9. **Any two from:** to produce goods and services; to meet customer needs; to add value [2]
10. **Possible answer:** An entrepreneur will need to have the required characteristics and skills to run a business [1]. This involves taking risks, being creative and the ability to make important decisions [1]. Enterprise is needed to organise the other factors of production to start a business [1].
11. Branding [1]; Quality [1]; Convenience [1]; Design [1]; Unique selling point [1]
12. **Possible answer:** Branding creates a well-known image for the good/service [1], making the business stand out from

competitors [1]. Customers are willing to pay a higher price for a branded good/service [1].

Page 14–15

1. **Any three from:** price; quality; choice; convenience; service
2. To satisfy the different wants of customers. Customers have different preferences.
3. The cost of a British Airways flight may include services that are optional with easyJet.
4. **Possible answers:** If customers' needs are met, they will purchase from the business, which will provide more revenue and potentially more profit for the business.
   Or
   They become loyal customers and repeat purchase, reducing the need for expensive advertising campaigns.
   Or
   They spread good news about the business to family and friends and provide good reviews, which raises the profile of the business and leads to new sales.

Pages 16–17

1. Market research is a process of collecting information about what consumers want, market trends and competitors.
2. Primary research; Secondary research
3. Quantitative data

Pages 18–19

1. Market segmentation involves breaking down a market into smaller groups (segments).
2. **Any four from:** location; demographics; lifestyle; income; age
3. A diagram used to position and compare products in a market.
4. **Any one from:** identify gaps in the market; awareness of the competition

Pages 20–21

1. A competitive environment is a market where there are many businesses selling similar goods and services.
2. **Any one from:** lower profits; businesses can find themselves in a price war; consumers may think the good or service is poor quality.
3. Businesses need to decide how they can meet customers' needs better than their competitors.

1. A [1]
2. **Possible answer:** New technology means a business can create innovative business ideas [1]. As a result, the business can meet changing customer needs such as convenience [1]. New goods and services can make tasks easier for customers [1] and they will be

prepared to pay a higher price [1]. This helps the business to recover expensive research and development costs [1]. Therefore the business will break-even faster [1].
3. **Possible answer:** By adding extra features to an existing product [1]. This improves what is available to customers [1] and helps to meet changing customer needs [1].
4. A [1]; C [1]
5. D [1]
6. **Possible answer:** Conducting market research [1] because careful planning to find out what customers want [1] will help to avoid bad business decisions [1].
7. **Possible answer:** Adding value increases the worth of a product [1]. A business must do this to cover the cost of producing its goods/services [1] and to ensure that it can make a profit [1].
8. **Possible answer:** A unique feature or design will make a good or service stand out from competitors [1] and attract customers [1] who will be willing to pay a higher price [1].

1. The needs and wants of customers when purchasing a product [1].
2. Customers have different tastes and preferences [1].
3. **Possible answer:** Through identifying customer needs, the business can meet them [1]. This is likely to generate sales [1] and ensure the survival of the business [1].
4. A [1]; E [1]
5. **Any one from:** Start-up businesses have a limited amount of money; Some market research methods are expensive; Market research requires specialist skills to get meaningful results [1]
6. **Possible answer:** Online reviews or comments about goods and services can determine what a customer thinks about a business's product or that of a competitor [1]. This data can be collected quickly and cheaply [1]. Therefore businesses can make decisions about their products and meet customer needs [1].
7. Quantitative data is numerical and can be measured easily [1].
8. C [1]; D [1]
9. **Possible answer:** Businesses need to focus their decisions on how they can make their products different from those of their competitors [1]. This will attract customers to their products [1]. Market research allows a business to keep a close eye on competitors [1] and enables it to find out what their customers want [1]. With this information, the business can change its approach (e.g. aspects of its products or pricing) to gain a competitive

advantage [1]. This can result in increased sales, leading to more profit [1].

Pages 26–27
1. The short-term steps the business will take in order to achieve its overall aim.
2. **Possible answers:** To allow the business to share its direction with staff so they know what to focus on and are motivated to perform, which drives productivity.
   Or
   To enable a business to measure its performance and therefore to help a business plan for the future, which reduces risk.
3. a) Any example that relates to money, e.g. profits.
   b) Any example that does not relate to money, e.g. personal challenge.

Pages 28–29
1. Fixed costs are costs that remain the same regardless of the level of output. Variable costs relate directly to the level of output and vary accordingly.
2. Fixed costs: rent or mortgage; salaries; insurance; marketing.
   Variable costs: raw materials; packaging; wages
3. How much each product made and sold contributes to fixed cost, then profit. Contribution = selling price per unit – variable costs per unit

Pages 30–31
1. A cash-flow forecast helps identify the timing of when, in the future, cash is paid into and out of a business.
2. **Any one from:** cash is critical to the survival of a business; cash prevents a business becoming insolvent; too much cash means that business is not earning any return.
3. Negotiating with suppliers for longer credit terms; Sending invoices to customers as soon as they place an order; Selling unwanted assets.

Pages 32–33
1. Short-term finance must be repaid within one year, whereas long-term finance can be repaid over a longer period of time.
2. **Possible answers:** A business can receive payment from its own customers before it pays the suppliers, removing the need for the business to raise its own finance and therefore maintaining a positive cash-flow.
   Or
   A business with low levels of cash can still get materials on a 'get now, pay later' scheme, which means works can still be undertaken, therefore reducing the likelihood of customer dissatisfaction on account of incomplete works.
3. Borrowing money from a bank by drawing more money than is actually in a current account, i.e. spending all of the business's money then dipping into the bank's money. Interest is charged by the bank on the amount overdrawn.

1. B [1]; C [1]
2. **Possible answer:** A successful business must understand what its customers want in advance in order to take advantage of demand at the earliest opportunity [1]. Keeping up to date with changes in fashion and taste is also important as customer needs continually change [1]. This helps the business to maximise sales and profit [1].
3. **Possible answer:** Market research can help an entrepreneur to identify gaps in the market [1], leading to opportunities for the business to satisfy customer needs that are not being met or that could be improved further [1]. As a result, a product can be created or amended that meets customer expectations and leads to higher sales for the business [1].
4. **Any two from:** more sales and revenue so greater profits; good customer reviews; repeat purchase/loyal customers [2]
5. Secondary market research uses data that already exists [1].
6. Interviews [1] or focus groups [1] in which open-ended questions can be asked to gain in-depth answers.
7. Breaking down the market into smaller groups (segments) [1].
8. To identify where a product will be placed in a market [1] compared to other similar products in the same market [1]. This allows a business to see how competitive the market is and if there are gaps in the market [1].
9. A gap in the market may have been identified because there is no demand for a particular product [1].
10. A [1]; E [1]
11. **Any one from:** buying cheaper raw materials to make cost savings [1]; offering exceptional customer service [1]; providing excellent quality [1]; offering promotions and loyalty discounts [1].

1. C [1]

   Helpful Tip
   Insurance is the only cost that will not change with an increase in output.

2. **Possible answer:** One financial objective of a business is to survive [1]. Many new small businesses will set this as its initial objective, as it has yet to establish a customer base and would have likely had high start-up costs, including land and machinery [1]. As a result, the business may aim to have enough cash at the end of the financial year to allow it to continue to trade [1].
   [Other answers could refer to profit, growth, sales, market share and financial security]
3. a) Break-even point = fixed costs ÷ contribution per unit [1]
      = £5000 ÷ (£15 – £5) = 500 [1]
   b) Margin of safety = total output – break-even point [1]
      = 1000 – 500 = 500 [1]

4. A [1]; E [1]

   Helpful Tip
   Both of these costs would increase on output.

5. **Any one from:** rent; raw materials; insurance; wages; salaries [1]
6. **Possible answer:** A long-term source of finance could come from a loan [1]. This is where the business borrows money from a bank, which it will need to repay with interest [1]. This means the business will need to pay more back than initially borrowed [1].
7. **Possible answer:** A short-term source of finance is trade credit [1]. This can be where you purchase raw materials from a supplier but you agree to pay them at a later date, e.g. within 30 days [1]. This reduces the cash outflow of the business for a short period of time, thus improving net cash-flow [1].
8. Percentage change = new amount – original amount; change ÷ original amount × 100 [1]
   = £16 000 – £15 000 = £1000;
   £1000 ÷ £15 000 × 100 = 6.67% [1]
9. **Possible answer:** A limitation of using share capital as a source of finance is that the existing owners lose some control of the business [1]. This means they have less decision-making power, as there are more shareholders involved in the decision making [1]. This could result in the business moving in a direction that was not intended by the original shareholders [1].
10. **Possible answer:** Having cash in a business will prevent it from becoming insolvent [1]. It will be able to continue to trade as it has cash available to pay for day-to-day expenses such as wages, rent and raw materials [1]. Without cash, the business would no longer be able to operate [1].

Pages 38–39
1. a sole trader; a partnership
2. **Any three from:** owner can lose personal possessions; hard to raise finance; owner can lose money if sick; owner can lose money if on holiday; high amount of tax if profit is high.
3. An arrangement between an established business (the franchisor) that allows other businesses or individuals (franchisees) the right to sell goods and services using its name, trademark and business processes.

Pages 40–41
1. **Any three from:** nature of the business; market; labour; materials; competitors
2. **Possible answers:** Customers will already shop in the location so a business can entice another's customers; Business can be another choice for customers if they decide to shop around.
3. **Possible answers:** The Internet has made it easier for some businesses to get started without the need for business premises; Buying and selling sites such as eBay, Etsy and Amazon are established online marketplaces; Customers can

find services through sites like Rated People; Businesses do not need to be located near to their customers; Sales can be made 24 hours a day, 7 days a week; New markets are available as the Internet allows a global reach.

Pages 42–43

1. Promotion
2. **Any one from:** A business may need to review its pricing strategy, offering a lower price to persuade customers to try their product; A business may need to review its product offering to differentiate themselves; A business may need a promotion campaign to remind customers of its relevance in the market; A business may need to look for alternative markets such as online to maintain market share.
3. **Possible answers:** The Internet gives customers access to information, making them more knowledgeable about prices, so some businesses have to change their prices to remain competitive.
   Or
   A business may be able to lower its prices due to cost savings made by technology.

Pages 44–45

1. The business idea, business aims and objectives, target market, forecast revenue, cost and profit, cash-flow forecast, sources of finance, location, marketing mix
2. **Any one from:** lenders; shareholders; owner; competition
3. **Any one from:** used to raise finance; to determine whether the business has a good chance of being successful; demonstrates that the entrepreneur has considered every aspect of the business; costly mistakes can be avoided if adequate research is undertaken; gives the business a plan with clear aims and objectives.

1. One reason why survival may be more important is that the new business is likely to have a high cash outflow for new machinery and may not have made many sales yet [1]. This means that it may struggle to have enough cash to pay for day-to-day expenses [1]. Therefore, survival may be more appropriate for a new business rather than looking to achieve profit early on [1].
2. An objective of a social enterprise will be a social objective, where it may feel passionate about a specific moral cause [1]. For example, some cosmetics businesses may believe it is not ethical to test products on animals [1]. Therefore, the business has produced a good or service while not harming the environment [1].
3. **Any two from:** cocoa; milk; sugar [2]
4. One reason why a business may become insolvent is due to a lack of cash inflow [1]. A business might not have made enough sales to pay for their day-to-day expenses [1]. A supplier can refuse to sell any more raw materials to the business. As a

result, the business can no longer trade, becoming insolvent [1].
5. **Any two from:** loan; mortgage; retained profit; share capital; venture capital [2]
6. a) $\frac{£10\,000}{(£8 - £4)}$ [1] = 2500 [1]
   b) 18\,000 – 2500 [1] = 15\,500 [1]
   c) 18\,000 × £8 = £144\,000
      18\,000 × £4 = £72\,000 [1]
      £144\,000 – (£72\,000 + £10\,000) = £62\,000 [1]
7. A benefit of using retained profit as a source of finance is that it is a cheap source of money [1]. Using money the company has already made in profit means that it does not have to pay interest on funds borrowed from a bank [1]. As a result, this lowers the overheads for the business [1].
8. A limitation of trade credit is that the business only has a small period of time in which to pay the money back to the supplier [1]. As a result, this does not improve a business's cash-flow position in the long term [1] and it is reliant on a good working relationship with the supplier [1].

1. A business owned by one person [1]
2. **Possible answer:** A sole trader (business owner) and their business are seen as one entity [1]. The owner has unlimited liability [1] and is at risk of losing personal possessions if the business incurs debts [1].
3. **Any one from:** more capital can be raised by a partner; partners bring a range of skills; problems and decisions are shared [1]
4. C [1]; D [1]
5. Businesses need to be where the raw materials are located [1].
6. Businesses need to be near suitably skilled staff who are willing to work for the wages/salaries that are being offered [1].
7. A [1]; D [1]
8. Place is about how businesses get products to customers when and where they are willing to buy them [1].
9. **Possible answer:** Businesses can use the Internet to sell their products [1] and target customers anywhere in the world [1]. Money can be saved by not needing physical business premises [1].
10. To help raise money from banks and other lenders [1].
11. B [1]; C [1]
12. **Possible answer:** It makes entrepreneurs look at all aspects of the business and address all areas [1]. Costly mistakes can be avoided as the business is well planned out [1], therefore reducing the risk when starting out [1].

Pages 50–51

1. A stakeholder is any person who has an interest in a business and is affected by the activities of a business.
2. **Any three from:** owners; managers; employees; shareholders; customers;

community; suppliers; government; competitors
3. **Any one from:** Customers seek quality for a fair price but owners want higher profits; Suppliers seek businesses able to pay bills on time but businesses may be trying to manage a cash-flow crisis; Staff want high wages but shareholders want high profits.

Pages 52–53

1. The activity of buying and selling goods and services online.
2. **Any one from:** lower manufacturing costs; lower waste; increased production times; increased cost of investment.
3. **Any one from:** Product: more technology now in many products; Price: reduced costs have helped reduce selling prices; Place: customers can buy online; Promotion: use of social media and online marketing.

Pages 54–55

1. Laws set by governments that set out a strict set of rules in which businesses can operate and individuals can act.
2. **Any two from:** discrimination; minimum wage; health and safety
3. Goods and services must be fit for purpose; As described; Of satisfactory quality.

Pages 56–57

1. The broad performance of a country's economy, measured by GDP.
2. **Possible answers:** Customers have less money to spend, which means they tend to buy cheaper products in lower quantities and this means prices might need to be lowered to remain competitive.
   Or
   The pool of available skilled workers increases, which means businesses are able to cherry-pick the best candidates and therefore be leaders in their field.
   Or
   Businesses don't have to offer such attractive pay packages, which can lower costs and therefore increase profit margins.
3. The amount charged for borrowing money or as a reward for saving.

Pages 58–59

1. **Any one from:** communication; access to research; speed of production; location
2. The Trading Standards Authority checks that businesses adhere to strict rules when selling goods and services. This protects the public from being sold counterfeit goods and therefore ensures a minimum level of quality.
3. Inflation is when the average price level increases.

1. **Any one from:** expensive to set up; other franchisees could damage their brand image; continued payment to the franchisor; cannot make own decisions [1]
2. The legal responsibility for an owner to pay the debts of a business [1].
3. **Any two from:** company accounts are published for the public to see [1]; lots of administration to get started [1]; shares cannot be sold to the public [1].

4. This gives business the opportunity to be an alternative choice if customers decide to shop around **[1]**.
5. **Possible answer:** A business can outsource its manufacturing to overseas locations **[1]**, which is often much cheaper **[1]**, therefore reducing fixed costs **[1]**.
6. **Possible answer:** If prices are too high, customers may choose to buy cheaper alternatives **[1]**, leading to fewer sales and revenue for a business **[1]**. This may lead to business failure **[1]**.
7. **Possible answer:** Customers' needs change all the time **[1]** and a business has to adapt its marketing mix **[1]** to keep up, such as by having special promotions to remain competitive in the market **[1]**.
8. New and cheaper promotion opportunities, such as by using email and social media **[1]**.
9. A document that summarises the future objectives of a business and shows how they will be achieved **[1]**.
10. **Possible answer:** A cash-flow forecast shows predicted monthly cash inflows and outflows **[1]**, allowing an entrepreneur to see when money may need to be borrowed to cover negative cash-flow **[1]**. Therefore, the business can ensure it is able to pay operating costs **[1]**.
11. They will want to see forecast revenue, costs and profit to determine if the business can pay back any money that is borrowed **[1]**.

1. A **[1]**

   Helpful Tip
   Employees work for the organisation.

2. C **[1]**

   Helpful Tip
   The promotion strategies of the business are within its control.

3. **Possible answer:** Banks can impact business activity by the interest rates that they set **[1]**. If a bank increases the interest rate of borrowing, this will increase the business's costs, as it will need to repay a greater amount **[1]**. This will decrease the business's profits owing to an increase in costs **[1]**.
4. **Possible answer:** A higher unemployment rate means that customers will have less money to spend on goods and services **[1]**. A decrease in spending is likely to reduce the total revenue of a business **[1]**, which will also reduce its profit **[1]**.
5. **Possible answer:** An increase in the value of the pound sterling means that a business can purchase the same number of goods and services from abroad for a lower price **[1]**. For a business, this means that total import costs will decrease **[1]**. As a result, the business will make more profit owing to a decrease in total costs **[1]**.

6. **Possible answer:** A consequence for a business not following employment law is that it will develop a poor reputation for managing staff **[1]**. This is likely to reduce motivation levels for current workers and may increase staff turnover **[1]**. The business may also face legal action and financial penalties **[1]**.
7. A **[1]**; B **[1]**
8. The products must be as described **[1]**, of reasonable quality and fit for purpose **[1]**.
9. **Possible answer:** Following consumer law will help a business to produce quality goods **[1]**. If products are of reasonable quality and fit for purpose, the business is likely to develop a good reputation and spend less time and money processing refunds **[1]**. This will help the business to increase sales revenue and profit **[1]**.
10. **Any two from:** e-commerce; social media; digital communication; payment systems **[2]**
11. **Possible answer:** Technology can impact the promotional strategies of the business **[1]**. Expanding its social media presence enables it to access customers more personally and cheaply than offline methods **[1]**. Updating its own social media pages is likely to cost less than methods such as newspaper or TV advertising **[1]**.
12. **Possible answer:** A government can ensure that the business is paying the right amount of tax **[1]**. An example of this is corporation tax, which is a charge on the profits of the business **[1]**. This means that the business keeps less profit at the end of the financial year **[1]**.

Pages 64–65
1. Organic growth is when a business grows on its own. Inorganic growth is when a business merges with (or takes over) another business.
2. It is cheaper because no interest is charged, which means fixed costs aren't increased.
3. It has to be repaid and is costly owing to interest being charged, which means fixed costs increase and profit falls.

Pages 66–67
1. **Any three from:** market conditions; economic climate; customer preference; technology; previous performance; legislation; stakeholder's vision
2. **Any three from:** focus on survival or growth; entering or exiting new markets; growing or reducing the workforce; increasing or decreasing the product range.
3. Where a business is breaking even, making just enough money to cover its costs.

Pages 68–69
1. When organisations and businesses trade internationally.
2. Imports are when products made overseas are brought into the UK. Exports

are when a business makes products in the UK then sells them to other countries.
3. A tariff is a tax that is added onto the selling price of an imported good, making it more expensive for importers to import into a country and therefore reducing competition from abroad.

Pages 70–71
1. Ethics are moral guidelines for good behaviour.
2. The majority of businesses operate to make profit. In order to make profit, businesses may need to produce goods and services cheaply, which might mean non-ethical behaviour such as paying wages that are below the legal requirement, and that creates an ethical conflict.
3. The main aim of a pressure group is to change the unethical activities of a business.

1. C **[1]**
2. **Possible answer:** One way an employee can impact the business is by influencing its brand image **[1]**. If an employee is motivated and productive, they are likely to produce consistently high-quality products **[1]**. This is likely to give the firm a competitive advantage, which can result in an increase in revenue **[1]**.
3. **Possible answer:** If technology, such as machinery to produce goods and services, is updated regularly then it is likely to result in an increase in productivity **[1]**. If a firm is using old technology, the production process is likely to be slower and the business might not be able to meet demand **[1]**. This could negatively affect customer service and the brand image of the business **[1]**.
4. **Possible answer:** An increase in minimum wage will increase the total wage costs for a firm **[1]**. Its profits are therefore likely to decrease owing to an increase in costs **[1]**. The business may then need to decide whether to raise the price of its products to maintain profit margins **[1]**.
5. **Any two from:** to be free of discrimination; to be given an employment contract; to not be asked to exceed working 48 hours a week; equal pay **[2]**
6. **Possible answer:** If a business ensures health and safety laws are met, it will reduce the risk of incurring fines or penalties **[1]**. Putting consumers or employees at harm can result in heavy fines, which increases the costs of the business **[1]** and results in less profit **[1]**.
7. **Possible answer:** If consumers have higher incomes, they will have more money to spend on goods and services **[1]**. As a result, a business is likely to see an increase in sales revenue owing to an increase in demand by consumers **[1]**. This is even more important to firms that sell luxury goods, like expensive holidays **[1]**.

8. a) $1500 \times \$20 = \$30\,000$ [1]

$$\frac{\$30\,000}{1.5} = £20\,000 \text{ [1]}$$

b) $\frac{\$30\,000}{1.80} = £16\,666.67$ [1]

$£20\,000 - £16\,666.67 = £3333.33$ [1]

9. **Possible answer:** A decrease in interest rates might increase the number of sales of a business [1]. If a consumer has to make smaller repayments on their borrowing, they have more of their income available to spend on goods and services [1]. This increases the likelihood of an increase in sales of a business [1].

10. **Possible answer:** A limitation of using social media is that it needs to be regularly updated to retain consumer interest [1]. This requires the business to employ workers to update the social media platforms [1], which increases its costs [1].

11. **Possible answer:** Digital communication increases the productivity of workers, as they are able to communicate more quickly using methods such as video calls [1]. An increase in productivity is likely to improve customer service [1] since the business is able to respond more efficiently to different parts of the production process [1].

Pages 74–75 Practice Questions

1. C [1]
2. **Possible answer:** A limitation of organic growth is that it tends to be slower than inorganic growth. [1]. This is because the business is growing internally, meaning that it will not be able to gain market share by merging or taking over a rival [1]. The business will need to increase market share by selling a new product or entering a new market, which takes a long time to research and create an appropriate set of strategies for [1].
3. **Possible answer:** A limitation of inorganic growth is that it is likely to be much more expensive than organic growth [1]. If a business wants to take over another company, it could involve huge amounts of spending [1]. This means the business would then have to find a method of finance that could involve borrowing, which increases its costs [1].
4. C [1]

> **Helpful Tip**
> Public limited companies allow investors to buy shares in the stock market.

5. **Possible answer:** A benefit of a public limited company is that it can gain huge amounts of capital needed through stock market flotation [1]. This is where the company will sell shares on the stock market that will allow investors to purchase [1]. All the money received from the purchase of the shares will go directly to the business that can be used for growth [1].

6. B [1]; D [1]
7. $£400\,000 \times (8 \div 100) = £32\,000$ [2]
   [1 mark for $400\,000 \times 8$]
8. **Possible answer:** A business's objectives may change over time due to an improved business performance from an increase in total revenue [1]. When a business is new, it is likely to try to achieve survival, owing to the high costs and lack of sales [1]. However, as the business becomes more established and increases its total revenue, it is more likely to set an objective of profit [1].
9. **Possible answer:** If the pound has weakened, a foreign customer can buy more UK-based products for a lower price [1]. As a result, this makes UK products more attractive to foreign buyers, leading to an increase in exports [1]. This means that the revenue of UK businesses is likely to increase [1].
10. **Possible answer:** A limitation of a trading bloc is that you cannot put tariffs on member states [1]. Tariffs are used to protect businesses from too many imports from foreign competition [1]. Without tariffs on fellow members, firms could suffer a decrease in sales due to increased competition [1].
11. **Possible answer:** A business might improve its brand image by being more ethical [1]. This enhanced brand image encourages more customers to purchase its goods and services [1], which increases the total revenue [1].

Pages 76–85 Revise Questions

Pages 76–77

1. Function; Aesthetics (appearance); Cost
2. Making changes to the product (re-branding, lower price); Appealing to a new market segment.
3. **Any three from:** brand image; unique selling point; offering a better location; features; function; design and appearance; cheaper selling price; quality; customer service; product range

Pages 78–79

1. **Any one from:** premium pricing; competition-based pricing; freemium pricing
2. **Any one from:** Digital products are offered for free with a premium for additional features, functionality or virtual goods; More discounts and comparison websites so prices need to be competitive; Better machinery and tools mean manufacturing is quicker, which saves costs and increases profit.
3. During introduction, the price helps to determine the value of a product, push sales or recover development and promotion costs. During the decline stage, a reduced price is a final try at achieving as many sales as possible.

Pages 80–81

1. Younger generations regularly use social media so advertising can be based on popular social media websites; more interactivity makes advertising more appealing to younger generations.

2. 'Buy one, get one free' can be used for mass market products as they are sold in high volumes.
3. **Any one from:** targeted advertising online; viral advertising via social media; e-newsletters

Pages 82–83

1. The location where customers can purchase goods and services.
2. A retailer has a physical location to sell their goods and services. An e-tailer sells their goods and services via the Internet.
3. **Any three from:** electronic transactions; global reach; meaningful suggestions; 24/7 purchase opportunity; sophisticated websites; personalised apps

Pages 84–85

1. An advantage held by a business that allows it to perform better than its competitors.
2. A high-priced, high-quality product will be promoted differently to a product that has a low price. This means it is unlikely that a luxury product would use a 'buy one, get one free' offer. instead, it may be preferable to pay for a magazine article highlighting features that would appeal to its target market.
3. Developing the correct balance between the elements of the market mix to build a successful marketing strategy and a competitive advantage.

Pages 86–87 Review Questions

1. A [1]
2. **Possible answer:** One benefit of increased market share is that the business has more price-setting power [1]. This is because it is likely to have strong customer loyalty owing to the repeated purchases of their products [1], which means that customers will be less sensitive to a change in price [1].
3. **Possible answer:** A business may choose to stay small for financial reasons [1]. The owner might not have the resources to finance business growth, such as by expanding the premises and employing more staff [1]. Taking out a loan from a bank would increase costs for the business [1].
4. B [1]
5. **Possible answer:** A limitation of a public limited company is the loss of control of who owns the business [1]. Once shares are sold in the business, those new investors can then sell their shares to the general public [1], which means the company cannot control new investors [1].
6. A [1]; C [1]
7. $£800\,000 \times (5 \div 100)$ [1]
   $= £40\,000$ [1]
8. **Possible answer:** A business may aim to achieve market growth in order to benefit from lower average costs [1]. When businesses buy products in bulk, they are able to negotiate discounts from suppliers [1], therefore lowering the variable costs for the business [1].
9. **Possible answer:** When the value of the pound increases, it results in imports

becoming cheaper **[1]** because importers can buy more foreign currency with the same number of pounds **[1]**. This means the business's costs will be lower owing to cheaper imports **[1]**.

10. **Possible answer:** A benefit of a trading bloc is that a business can target more customers in that region **[1]**. The removal of tariffs makes it cheaper for foreign customers to purchase domestic products **[1]**, resulting in an increase in total revenue **[1]**.

11. **Possible answer:** A trade-off of a business being more ethical is that it may result in an increase in total costs **[1]**. For example, if a business hired someone to improve the welfare of its employees **[1]**, there would be another salary to pay, increasing its fixed costs **[1]**.

12. **Possible answer:** One reason why selling assets may not be useful is that the business may need to use those assets in the future **[1]**. For example, a business may sell old machinery that has decreased in value **[1]** but if new machinery is later needed to do the same job, it is likely to be more expensive **[1]**.

Pages 88–89 **Practice Questions**

1. D **[1]**
2. **Any two from:** research and development; introduction; growth; maturity; saturation; decline **[2]**
3. The cost of making a product **[1]**; The demand for a product **[1]**
4. It means a business may have to reduce its prices to remain competitive in the market as customers have choice if they think a product is priced too high **[1]**.
5. Freemium pricing allows businesses to offer digital products for free, which attracts customers **[1]** after they have used the digital product. The business can offer additional features or functionality, which will be charged **[1]**. Therefore, the business can make revenue **[1]**.
6. Customers must be able to afford the products. If the price is set too high, products may not sell and a business will make little revenue **[1]**.
7. Promotion is about communicating that a product is available and is a way of persuading new and existing customers to make a purchase **[1]**.
8. **Any two from:** website advertising; social media; e-mail adverts; banner adverts; pop-ups; apps **[2]**
9. Customers need to be able to purchase products in a place that they want **[1]**.
10. **Any one from:** more interactive; captivating; links in the e-newsletter can direct customers to where businesses want them to go **[1]**.
11. Some customers may be reluctant to pay for items over the Internet **[1]**, for example owing to concern about the possibility of fraud **[1]**. Therefore, they may opt to shop with businesses that have a physical location, which reduces the competitiveness of the e-tailer **[1]**.

12. Competitive advantage is a benefit that allows a business to perform better than its competitors **[1]**.
13. If customers demand a low-priced product **[1]**, a business will need to produce it using cheaper raw materials **[1]**. This could result in a low-quality product **[1]**.

Pages 90–97 **Revise Questions**

Pages 90–91
1. To create goods and services
2. Job production; Batch production; Flow production
3. Lower costs; Increased productivity; Improved quality; Further flexibility

Pages 92–93
1. Maximum stock level; Minimum stock level (buffer stock); Re-order level; Lead time; Order quantity
2. Just in time stock control is where businesses do not hold any stock. Raw materials and components are ordered in exactly when they are needed and are used straight away in the production process.
3. Quality; Delivery; Availability; Cost; Trust

Pages 94–95
1. Meeting a minimum set of standards to satisfy customer expectations for a good or service.
2. Quality control
3. **Any one from:** Quality is checked at every part of the production process; Every worker takes responsibility for quality; Zero-defect production.

Pages 96–97
1. Product knowledge; Efficiency of service; Customer engagement; Customer feedback; Post-sales service.
2. **Any one from:** loyal customers that repeat purchase; hard for competitors to take customers; good reviews; more sales; a positive working environment; good reputation and brand; a competitive advantage
3. **Possible answers:** Customer complaints can results in a loss of sales and/or negative reviews, leading to a bad reputation for the business.
Or
Staff may require retraining, which increases the costs of the business and they may need to be passed on to the consumer in the form of increased prices.

Pages 98–99 **Review Questions**

1. The capabilities of a product to perform its intended purpose **[1]**.
2. To prevent a product going into decline **[1]**.
3. **Possible answer:** Research, design and development costs are high **[1]** and sales are low **[1]** as customers have little awareness of the product **[1]**. A lot of money will be spent on promotion during this stage **[1]** because a business will be trying to persuade customers to make a purchase **[1]**. High costs and low sales mean the business will be making a loss **[1]**.

4. A **[1]**; B **[1]**
5. The browsing habits of customers can be collected through Internet cookies and promotions can then be targeted towards what they usually look at online **[1]**.
6. The route that a product takes, from where it is manufactured to where it is sold **[1]**.
7. **Any one from:** free parking; product warranty; customer service **[1]**
8. **Possible answer:** Convenience **[1]**, as customers can shop at anytime from anywhere **[1]** and do not have to go to a physical shop **[1]**.
9. **Any two from:** the business's objectives; the market; the size of the business; the competition; the nature of the product **[2]**

Pages 100–101 **Practice Questions**

1. **Any one from:** products are high quality; they are unique and tailored to meet customer needs; workers are motivated and take pride in their work; a business can charge a high price **[1]**.
2. **Possible answer:** A breakdown in one of the lines impacts the entire production process **[1]**. The entire assembly line may need to be stopped to enable any faults to be rectified **[1]**, meaning there could be a delay in sending out customers' orders **[1]**.
3. **Possible answer:** Machines and robots work autonomously **[1]**, unlike workers who need breaks, holidays and time off **[1]**. Therefore, a business can produce more units in a shorter time period **[1]**.
4. **Any two from:** raw materials; stock of materials that are not yet completed (work in progress); finished goods **[2]**
5. The lowest amount of stock that a business wishes to hold at any one time **[1]**.
6. **Possible answer:** Supplier relations need to be strong and flexible **[1]**, since this ensures that stock can be ordered at short notice **[1]** yet still arrive in good time and be of good quality **[1]**.
7. Quality will be high, meaning less wastage from defective products **[1]**.
8. **Possible answer:** Staff need to know how to effectively check that products are meeting the minimum standards **[1]**. All staff need to have the same standards **[1]** to ensure there are no inconsistencies in the quality checking process **[1]**.
9. Customer feedback (both positive and negative) can tell a business how customers feel about its products **[1]**.
10. Procedures that a business has in place to support customers after the sale of a good or service **[1]**.
11. **Possible answer:** Customers may leave negative reviews of the business **[1]**.

Pages 102–105 **Revise Questions**

Pages 102–103
1. Gross profit is sales revenue – cost of sales. Net profit is gross profit – operating costs and interest.

2. Profitability looks at how good a business is at making a profit. Profit is how much profit the business has made.

3. Average rate of return is (total profit ÷ number of years) ÷ cost of investment × 100

   Average rate of return calculates how much an entrepreneur or investor is getting back annually on the money they invested.

Pages 104–105

1. Numerical and statistical data

2. Marketing data is data a business collects to help make decisions. Market data refers to information that relates to a variety of investment markets.

3. **Any three from:** it may only be a snapshot of a certain period of time; it can quickly become out of date; it may be inaccurate as the data collected may be biased or might have missed out vital contributing factors; two people reading the same quantitative data may have different ways of understanding it.

1. **Any two from:** job production; flow production; batch production **[2]**

2. **Possible answer:** Similar items are grouped and made together (in batches) **[1]**. More products can be made at one time **[1]**, so the cost per unit is lower **[1]**.

3. **Possible answer:** A reliable supplier ensures orders are delivered on time **[1]**, allowing businesses to meet demand and produce good quality products for their customers **[1]**. This ensures customer satisfaction **[1]**.

4. The act of obtaining or buying raw materials, components or services from a supplier to be used in the production of goods and services **[1]**.

5. **Any two from:** costs involved in storage space; insurance; security; employing staff to manage storage; interest on borrowing used to buy stock **[2]**

6. **Possible answer:** Every worker is responsible for quality **[1]**, which involves workers in decision making **[1]**, increasing their levels of motivation **[1]**.

7. **Possible answer:** Good quality products meet customers' expectations **[1]**. Happy customers make repeat purchases and recommend goods and services to friends and family **[1]**, which then leads to further word-of-mouth sales **[1]**.

8. Product knowledge enables a sales person to effectively communicate the features and benefits of products, ensuring they match the most appropriate product to the customer **[1]**.

9. **Possible answer:** Cost is important as a business will wish to pay the lowest price possible for raw materials **[1]**. If a business can buy in bulk, suppliers may offer a discount **[1]**. This allows a business to keep costs low and may enable it to offer a lower price to customers **[1]**.

1. **Possible answer:** One way in which a business could increase gross profit is by advertising **[1]**. As more consumers become aware of the products or services offered by a business, more sales are likely to result **[1]**. If total revenue increases, then the gross profit will also increase (total revenue – cost of sales) **[1]**.

2. **Any two from:** insurance; advertising; rent; salaries **[2]**

3. a) Net profit = gross profit – overheads
   £8000 – £5000 **[1]** = £3000 **[1]**
   b) Gross profit margin = gross profit ÷ revenue × 100
   £8000 ÷ £18 000 × 100 **[1]** = 44.4% **[1]**

4. **Possible answer:** The net profit margin might have decreased due to an increase in overheads **[1]**. An example of an overhead is rent **[1]**. If the owner of the property increases the price of rent for the business, then this increases their costs, which in turn decreases the net profit margin for a business **[1]**.

5. Cost of sales = £45 000 – £15 000 = £30 000 **[1]**
   Net profit = £15 000 – £10 000 = £5000 **[1]**

6. a) $\frac{£20\,000}{£50\,000} \times 100$ **[1]** = 40% **[1]**

   b) Net profit = gross profit – expenses
   £20 000 – £10 000 = £10 000 **[1]**
   Net profit margin = net profit ÷ total revenue × 100
   $\frac{£10\,000}{£50\,000} \times 100$ = 20% **[1]**

7. ARR = average annual profit ÷ initial investment × 100
   $\frac{£5000}{£40\,000} \times 100$ **[1]** = 12.5% **[1]**

Pages 110–111

1. An organisational structure is the internal structure of a business and the roles and responsibilities of the staff who work for it, shown in levels of authority.

2. A centralised structure is where big decisions are made by senior management in a head office. In decentralised structures business decisions are made at a local level by local management.

3. People working away from the business, whether from home or even in different countries.

Pages 112–113

1. Hierarchy is the organisational structure of a business that allows everyone to see who is responsible for what role. Senior management sits at the top of the hierarchy. Middle management, team leaders and supervisors are in the middle of the hierarchy. Workers are at the bottom of the hierarchy.

2. **Any two from:** new recruits are often highly motivated; new recruits are often highly productive; new recruits bring new ideas.

3. CV; job description; person specification; job application form

Pages 114–115

1. When a business arranges for staff to have training that has specific objectives.

2. When an employee studies without the presence of a teacher or colleague.

3. **Possible answers:** Staff are more likely to feel appreciated, which is motivating and likely to increase productivity.
   Or
   Staff know how to do their job well and therefore enjoy their roles, resulting in better performance.
   Or
   Staff know how to do their job well and therefore make fewer mistakes, resulting in lower costs.

Pages 116–117

1. When staff want to give their best effort and care about the business they work for.

2. **Any three from:** attract new recruits; word-of-mouth recommendations can save costs on recruitment; lower absenteeism; reduced staff turnover; improved customer service; increased productivity; increased quality of work

3. The perks of a business, such as the use of a company car or free gym membership.

1. **Possible answer:** A limitation of financial data is that it could be out of date **[1]**. If the information is more than a year old, it may no longer be representative of the performance of a business or individual market **[1]**. As a result, the business may act upon incorrect information, leading to poor decisions **[1]**.

2. **Possible answer:** A benefit of using average rate of return is that it helps a business decide on whether to invest in a project **[1]**. Calculating whether the investment is viable or not can save/ make the business a significant amount of money **[1]**. If the project is not viable, then the business will not waste resources on the project **[1]**.

3. a) Cost of sales = £100 000 – £70 000 = £30 000
   Overheads = £70 000 – £30 000 **[1]** = £40 000 **[1]**
   b) £70 000 ÷ £100 000 × 100 **[1]** = 70% **[1]**
   c) £30 000 ÷ £100 000 × 100 **[1]** = 30% **[1]**

4. Profit per year = £100 000 ÷ 5 = £20 000
   £20 000 ÷ £200 000 × 100 **[1]** = 10% **[1]**

5. **Possible answer:** A business can use the profitability ratios to compare performance against competitors / previous years' performances **[1]**.

6. £5 – £2.50 = £2.50
   £2.50 × 50 000 = £125 000 **[1]**
   £125 000 – £25 000 = £100 000 **[1]**

7. Total revenue = £80 000 + £150 000 = £230 000 **[1]**
   Overheads = £150 000 – £100 000 = £50 000 **[1]**

1. **Possible answer:** A centralised organisational structure is when the majority of decisions are made by those at the top of the organisational hierarchy [1]. As a result, less staff are involved in decision making, which means that decisions are made more efficiently [1]. This leads to more productivity due to the speed of decision making [1].
2. **Possible answer:** One impact of appointing temporary staff is that they can be used to deal with a sudden increase in seasonal demand [1]. When there may be more demand around a period like Christmas, the business can hire more staff to maximise sales [1]. Once the busy period is over, the business can release the temporary staff [1].
3. **Possible answer:** A benefit of a decentralised organisational structure is that more employees have autonomy in decision making [1], which makes them feel more motivated [1]. As the business makes them feel more valued, they are more likely to be productive [1].
4. A [1]
5. **Possible answer:** One impact of remote working is that staff turnover is likely to decrease [1]. If employees have other commitments like childcare, then flexible working allows them to meet their personal needs and still allows them to continue their job role [1]. Keeping staff reduces the expense of recruiting new staff and training them, which lowers the cost for the business [1].
6. A [1]
7. C [1]
8. **Possible answer:** A limitation of internal recruitment is that the existing employees may not have the skills required to do the job role that is advertised [1]. As a result, the business would have to spend time and money to develop their skills [1], which is unproductive time from the business's point of view [1].
9. **Possible answer:** A limitation of external recruitment is that you only have a limited period of time in the interview process to determine if the employee would be appropriate for the business [1]. They will naturally want to be seen in their best light and that might not be a true reflection of their normal job performance [1]. This means the firm might hire an unproductive member of staff [1].
10. **Possible answer:** A financial method to motivate workers could be commission [1]. Paying staff based on the number of sales that they make can motivate them to be more productive [1]. This is likely to result in increased sales for the business but also increased income for a productive worker [1].
11. A [1]
12. **Possible answer:** A non-financial method of increasing motivation is job rotation [1]. Changing the roles of the employees will prevent them from having to constantly repeat the same tasks and potentially getting bored. [1]. As a result of being given different roles regularly, their motivation is likely to increase [1].

1. **Possible answer:** One purpose of a person specification is that it lets the potential applicant know the skills required for the job [1]. This allows the candidate to determine whether they meet the requirements [1]. If they do not then they will not apply, which saves the business time when filtering candidates in the selection process [1].
2. **Possible answer:** One barrier to effective communication is the use of technical jargon [1]. If a business uses lots of technical words, some of the employees may not understand the meaning of them [1]. This is likely to result in a decrease in productivity [1].
3. **Possible answer:** A benefit of a motivated workforce is that the staff are more likely to be productive [1]. This is because they enjoy their work and will increase efficiency when completing required tasks [1]. An increase in productivity can lower average costs for the business [1].
4. A [1]
5. **Possible answer:** A limitation of formal training is that it means that staff are not being productive in the period of the training session [1]. This means that the business's costs will rise due to the cost of training and the lack of productivity of staff [1]. This results in a reduction in profitability [1].
6. **Possible answer:** A limitation of a centralised organisational structure is that the majority of staff are not involved in the decision-making process, which can decrease their motivation [1]. As a result of a decrease in motivation staff are more likely to call in sick [1]. This results in a decrease in productivity [1].
7. **Possible answer:** A limitation of a decentralised organisational structure is that decision making could be a lot less efficient [1]. This is because more people are involved in the decision-making process and therefore more input means that the decisions will take longer [1]. This results in a decrease in productivity [1].
8. **Possible answer:** Technology is constantly evolving, so if employees are not equipped to use the technology, it will lead to a decrease in productivity [1]. If staff know how to use the technology then this will mean better customer service [1], which will increase the brand image of the business [1].
9. B [1]
10. C [1]
11. **Possible answer:** A limitation of financial methods of motivation is that it increases costs [1]. If an employee is paid commission and increases sales it means that the business's costs increase [1]. They may have made these sales anyway so the business might not receive any financial benefit [1].
12. **Possible answer:** Some workers might not be motivated by non-financial methods, such as job rotation, because performing the other roles might not increase motivation [1].

1. **Possible answer:** A benefit of 'just in time' production is that it reduces storage costs [1]. As stock is only ordered when required, it is likely to result in less wastage [1], which reduces the business's variable costs [1].
2. **Possible answer:** An appropriate objective for an established business is growth [1]. The business has already proved to be successful and may have built up some retained profit that could be used to expand the business to new markets [1]. This would result in an increase in brand awareness and profits [1].
3. **Possible answer:** A decrease in the unemployment rate could lead to an increase in sales for a business [1]. As consumers have a higher disposable income, they are able to purchase more goods and services [1], which means it could increase the total revenue [1].
4. **Possible answer:** A benefit of using retained profit as a source of finance is that you do not need to pay the money back or any interest repayments [1]. This lower costs for the business [1] because there are no repayments required for borrowing [1].
5. **Possible answer:** A limitation of quantitative data is that it does not provide explanations for answers [1]. For example, if someone was asked in a questionnaire with a closed response whether they enjoyed their experience, it will not tell the researcher why they enjoyed the experience or not [1]. This means the data is limited and the business might not be able to act upon it [1].
6. **Possible answer:** A purpose of setting a break-even point is to help the business determine an appropriate selling price [1]. If the business calculates that it has to make a significant number of sales to break even, it can increase its prices to break even more quickly [1]. This enables the business to make better financial decisions [1].
7. **Possible answer:** The purpose of creating a marketing map is to help identify a gap in the market [1]. If the business can identify a customer need that is not currently being met then it can help create a unique selling point [1], which can increase the revenue for the business [1].
8. **Possible answer:** A benefit of good communication is that staff will feel more motivated [1] as they are given clear information on how to fulfil their role [1]. As a result, this is likely to increase productivity, which lowers average costs [1].
9. **Possible answer:** A limitation of quality assurance is that it increases the costs of the business [1]. This is because they will

need to employ someone to inspect the quality of the products at every stage of production [1]. This increases the wage costs [1].

10. **Possible answer:** A business must keep financial records for legal reasons [1]. The government requires to see the accounts of a business to determine the appropriate amount of tax that it will need to pay [1]. This ensures the business is abiding by the law [1].

11. **Possible answer:** A limitation of a tall organisational structure is that communication will take longer, which slows down productivity [1]. If there are too many layers, messages will take longer to pass down the hierarchy [1] and this can also negatively affect motivation [1].

12. **Possible answer:** A benefit of quality assurance is that the quality of goods and services are likely to improve, as the products have been checked at every stage of production [1]. This means that customers are more likely to be satisfied with the product [1], increasing the brand image of the business [1].

13. **Possible answer:** There may be a conflict between employees and the shareholders [1]. This is because the shareholders want to maximise profits, but the employees want higher wages. [1] The more the business pays their employees the higher their costs, which lowers the profits made by the shareholders [1].

14. **Possible answer:** A tariff reduces the total amount of imports of foreign products through charging a tax [1]. As a result, a decrease in the purchase of foreign goods and services may persuade consumers to switch to cheaper UK goods and services [1]. This increases the tax revenue for the government [1].

15. **Possible answer:** An increase in inflation means that raw materials and wages are likely to increase [1]. This will

result in a decrease in profit [1] owing to an increase in total costs [1].

16. **Possible answer:** E-commerce could reduce the costs of the business as it would not need a physical store [1]. Running costs such as rent and utilities are likely to decrease [1], which helps to improve profitability [1].

17. **Possible answer:** It is important for a business to differentiate its products so that it can gain a competitive advantage [1]. In a hotly contested market, it is important to make sure the products stand out from the competition [1] to give them the best chance of delivering an increase in revenue [1].

18. £20 000 – £12 000 = £8000 [1]
£8000 + £4000 = £12 000 [1]

19. **Possible answer:** One risk of running a business is business failure [1]. If the business is not successful it may not make the required sales to prevent insolvency. [1] As a result, if the business has unlimited liability it could result in a loss of personal wealth [1].

20. **Possible answer:** If a consumer's income increases, it means that they are able to buy more goods and services [1]. As a result, they are likely to be less price sensitive if a business decides to increase their prices [1]. This means that the business would be advised to increase prices if incomes rise [1].

21. D [1]

22. **Possible answer:** A benefit of a trading bloc is that it gives a business a much wider target audience to aim its products at [1]. This means that it could sell more goods and services to consumers inside the trading bloc but not in the UK [1]. This will result in an increase in total revenue for the business [1].

23. C [1]

24. **Possible answer:** It is important to retain staff as it reduces the costs of the business [1]. Replacing employees who leave costs money in terms of advertising the job and training a new

employee [1], resulting in an increase in total costs [1].

25. **Possible answer:** A freelance worker might only be needed for a single event and therefore it would not be cost effective to hire them permanently [1]. For example, a photographer for a business event would not need to be retained after the event [1], as it would increase costs for little productivity [1].

26. **Possible answer:** A business will have buffer stock levels in order to improve customer service [1]. If a business does not run out of stock, then customers will be able to purchase the products when required [1]. This means customer service levels remain high, resulting in an increase in total revenue [1].

27. **Possible answer:** A business may choose to be more ethical to improve its brand image [1]. If customers perceive that the business is sustainable and considers their well-being then they are more likely to purchase its products [1], which results in an increase in total revenue [1].

28. **Possible answer:** A business may choose to relocate its production to another country in order to reduce costs [1]. In the UK, the minimum wage might be higher than the labour costs abroad [1], so by relocating, the business can produce its products at a lower cost [1].

29. **Possible answer:** An increase in legislation is likely to lead to an increase in total cost [1]. If the government changes a regulation such as a new health and safety law, the business will need to pay for training [1] to raise staff awareness, which increases cost [1].

30. **Possible answer:** One purpose of a business plan is to try and gain investment to help the business grow [1]. If a business wants to borrow money from a bank, the bank will need to see the business plan to determine whether it is a safe investment or not [1]. This will help the bank to determine whether or not to provide a loan [1].

31. C [1]

Formulae to Learn for the Exam

Total variable cost
Total variable cost = variable cost per unit × quantity

Total costs
TC (total cost) = TFC (total fixed costs) + TVC (total variable costs)

Revenue
Revenue = price × quantity

Break even
$$\text{Break-even point in units} = \frac{\text{fixed costs}}{(\text{sales price} - \text{variable cost per unit})}$$

Break-even point in costs / revenue = break-even point in units × sales price

Margin of safety
Margin of safety = actual or budgeted sales − break-even sales

Interest (on loans)
$$\text{Interest (on loans) in \%} = \frac{\text{total repayment} - \text{borrowed amount}}{\text{borrowed amount}} \times 100$$

Net cash-flow
Net cash-flow = cash inflows − cash outflows in a given period

Opening and closing balances
Opening balance = closing balance of the previous period

Closing balance = opening balance + net cash-flow

Profit
Profit = total revenue − total cost

Gross profit
Gross profit = sales revenue − cost of sales

Gross profit margin
$$\text{Gross profit margin (\%)} = \frac{\text{gross profit}}{\text{sales revenue}} \times 100$$

Net profit
Net profit = gross profit − other operating expenses and interest

Net profit margin
$$\text{Net profit margin (\%)} = \frac{\text{net profit}}{\text{sales revenue}} \times 100$$

Average rate of return
$$\text{Average rate of return (\%)} = \frac{\text{average annual profit (total profit} \div \text{number of years)}}{\text{cost of investment}} \times 100$$

Glossary

Added value: the increased worth that a business creates for a product; it is the difference between what a business pays its suppliers and the price that it is able to charge for the good/service.

Advertising Standards Authority (ASA): a body that ensures all advertising claims are accurate and true so consumers are not misled.

Aims: the long-term goals of an organisation.

Appraisals: when members of staff meet with their line manager to review their work over a period of time.

Assets: something of value to the business, such as machinery or land.

Autonomy: when a member of staff is given freedom to make decisions, they are given autonomy.

Average rate of return (ARR): calculates how much an entrepreneur or investor is getting back on the money invested in a business so they know how profitable their investment is.

Bank: an institution that provides businesses with financial services, which include providing loans and allowing them to save money.

Bar gate stock graph: a stock control diagram used to determine when new materials should be re-ordered.

Batch production: a production process in which similar components or goods are made together in groups (batches).

Biometrics: biological measurements or physical characteristics that can be used to identify a person.

Bonus: addition to the basic wage or salary, e.g. for achieving a target.

Boycott: when customers avoid a business because they disapprove of its actions.

Brand: a named product that consumers see as being different from other products and which they can associate and identify with.

Break even: the level of output where total revenues are equal to total costs; this is where neither a profit nor loss is being made, i.e. how many units need to be sold to cover all costs but not yet make a profit.

Business location: the place where a business operates.

Business ownership: the different legal structures of a business.

Business plan: a plan for the development of a business, detailing how the business will achieve its goals.

Capital: another name for money.

Cash-flow: the flow of cash into and out of a business.

Cash-flow forecast: making a prediction of the future cash inflows and outflows of a business, usually over the period of a month.

Cash inflow: the flow of cash into a business, e.g. from sales/sale of assets/raising capital.

Cash outflow: the flow of cash out of a business to pay, e.g. salaries, rent, suppliers.

Centralised: businesses with many branches (such as restaurant chains/retail shops) prefer big decisions to be made by senior management in a head office, which all branches then follow.

Click-through rate: the number of people who visit a web page who click on a hypertext link to a further website, usually for sales purposes.

Closing balance: the amount of money a business has in its account at the end of a period of time, e.g. a month, a financial year.

Commission: payment system usually operated for sales staff where their earnings are determined by how much they sell.

Commodities: raw materials such as oil, wheat, metals, coffee.

Companies House: in the UK, the official government organisation that keeps a record of all UK companies and information about them. A company that wishes to become a limited company must, by law, be registered with Companies House.

Competition law: regulations made by the government to ensure that fair competition is sustained; it also prevents businesses implementing anti-competitive strategies to force a competitor out of the market.

Competitive advantage: an advantage a business has that enables it to perform better than its rivals in the market and which is both distinctive and defensible.

Competitive environment: a market where there are many businesses selling similar goods and services.

Computer aided design (CAD): using computers in the design or modelling process of components or goods.

Computer aided manufacture (CAM): using computers to control machines and equipment.

Consumer: the person who ultimately uses (or consumes) a product.

Consumer income: the amount of money consumers have left to spend after they have paid their taxes and living expenses.

Consumer Rights Act: an Act that protects the public's buying rights when purchasing goods and services.

Consumer spending: the amount of money consumers have to spend.

Contribution per unit: how much each product made and sold contributes to fixed cost, then profit. Contribution = selling price per unit – variable costs per unit.

Cost of goods sold: costs directly linked with the production of goods or services; the more products or services sold, the higher the variable costs will be. Also known as **direct costs**.

Costs: the expenses and bills a business has to pay.

Crowdfunding: when a business attracts a crowd of investors from the Internet, each of whom takes a small stake by contributing towards an online fundraising target.

Customers: any individuals or organisations who buy or are supplied with a product by a business.

Customer engagement: the means by which a business creates a connection between its customer base and the experiences of customers with the business.

Customer needs: the wants and desires of buyers of a product or the customers of a business.

Customer reviews: information direct from customers, of their thoughts and feelings about a product or service.

CV: a document an applicant creates that is a summary of their personal, career, education and skills details.

Decentralised: where business decisions are made at a local level, by local managers rather than centrally by senior managers.

Decline phase: the final phase of the product life cycle; products become outdated as tastes and technology change.

Demographics: statistical data relating to the population and particular groups within it.

Design mix: the range of variables that contribute to successful design – they are function, cost and appearance.

Development: improving or perfecting existing skills.

Differentiation: making a product/service different from another in some way.

Digital communication: communicating using electronic equipment such as emails, texts, websites.

Direct costs: costs directly linked with the production of goods or services; the more products or services sold, the higher the variable costs will be. Also known as **cost of goods sold**.

Directors: individuals responsible for companies.

Discrimination: when individuals are treated differently based on their age, race, religion, gender or disability.

Distribution: to get a product to the right place for customers to make their purchases.

Distribution channel: the route that a product takes, from where it is manufactured to where it is sold.

Dividend: a sum of money paid regularly by a company to its shareholders out of its profits.

Dynamic business: businesses that adapt to meet the changing needs of customers and developments in the market.

E-commerce: the activity of buying and selling goods and services online.

Economic climate: the broad performance of the UK economy.

Economies of scale: cost advantages gained by expanding the level of production.

Employees: a person who is hired for a wage, salary, fee or payment to perform work for an employer or business.

Employment laws: regulations created by the government to protect the welfare of employees.

End user: the consumer or person who ultimately uses a product.

E-newsletter: a newsletter published electronically.

E-tailer: businesses that sell goods and services through the Internet.

Enterprise: the characteristics and skills needed to start a business and take risks.

Entrepreneur: a person who owns and runs their own business and takes risks.

Environmental laws: regulations created by the government to ensure that business practices are sustainable and limit damage to the environment.

Ethics: moral guidelines for good behaviour; doing what is morally right.

Exchange rate: the cost of exchanging one currency for another.

Exports: when a business makes products in the UK then sells them to other countries.

Extension strategies: methods used by businesses to prolong the sales of their products, e.g. rebranding, lower price.

External recruitment: when a business hires people from outside the business.

External source of finance: finance that is obtained from outside the business, such as bank loans and cash from the issue of shares.

Factors of production: the resources required by an entrepreneur to produce goods and services.

Financial data: past, present and future records of the financial health of a business. This could include financial and accounting records as well as sales, marketing and salary data.

Financial security: being financially independent and not having to rely on others for income.

Fixed costs: costs that remain the same regardless of the level of output, e.g. salaries, advertising, rent.

Flat (organisation): few levels of authority in a business.

Flexible hours: when someone will work the number of hours they are contracted to but with more choice over when they work.

Flow production: a large number of identical components or goods produced together on an assembly line.

Formal training: when a business arranges for staff to have training that has specific objectives. Formal training is provided by specialists and tends to be away from work.

Franchise: the right given by one business to another to sell goods or services using its name.

Franchisee: a business that agrees to manufacture, distribute or provide a branded product, under licence from a franchisor.

Franchisor: the business that gives franchisees the right to sell its product in return for a fixed sum of money or a royalty payment.

Freelance contracts: when someone is self-employed and they choose to work for different businesses on a contract-by-contract basis.

Freemium: a pricing strategy offering an initial product or service for free but which requires a payment for any additional services that are deemed premium.

Fringe benefits: when a business rewards its staff with something of financial value such as the use of a company car, free gym membership or free travel.

Full-time: with regards to employment, staff who work for around 35 hours per week.

Gap in the market: occurs when no business is currently serving the needs of customers for a particular product.

Give notice: when an employee or employer advises the other that they wish to terminate the employment contract.

Globalisation: when organisations and businesses trade internationally.

Goods: physical, tangible products, such as a car, a pair of scissors or a smart phone.

Government: the people and organisations given the authority to govern a country.

Gross Domestic Product (GDP): an estimate of the total value of goods and services produced in a country.

Gross profit: a calculation of how much profit a business makes from selling products or services after it has deducted the cost of sales (costs incurred directly). The formula for gross profit is: sales revenue – cost of sales.

Gross profit margin: the percentage of sales revenue that is left once the cost of sales has been paid; the formula for gross profit margin is: gross profit ÷ sales revenue × 100.

Growth: when a business becomes bigger.

Growth phase: the second phase of the product life cycle; sales grow as awareness of the product and its popularity increases.

Hierarchical: something that relates to levels of authority.

Incorporation: a registered company. Owners have limited liability.

Indirect costs: costs not directly linked with the production of the good or service being produced and sold.

Informal training: when a business arranges for staff to receive less structured training. Informal training usually takes place within the workplace and involves other team members to provide training.

Imports: when products made overseas are brought into the UK.

Inflation: when prices of goods and services continue to rise.

Inorganic growth: happens when a business conducts a merger (when two businesses join together) or takeover. Also known as external growth.

Insolvency: when a business does not have enough cash to pay its bills when they are due.

Interest rate: the amount charged for borrowing money or as a reward for savings.

Internal recruitment: when a business decides to appoint someone for a job who already works for the business.

Internal source of finance: when a business finds the money from within itself, such as retained profit or the sale of assets.

Internet cookies: data collected by a website and stored on a user's computer that allows the browsing history to be collected so preferences can be applied on future visits.

Introduction phase: the first phase of the product life cycle; the launch of the product.

Jargon: the vocabulary used by an industry/profession/group of people that relates to their area of expertise.

Job application form: form prepared by a business for a candidate to complete when applying for a job.

Job description: a document prepared by a business that explains the responsibilities and duties of a job and the day-to-day tasks related to the job.

Job enrichment: when a business tries to make a job more demanding and less boring in order to motivate staff.

Job production: a production method where one component or good is produced at a time.

Job rotation: staff are given short periods of time on various jobs before they move onto other jobs.

Just in time (JIT): a stock management system where stock is delivered only when needed by the production system, so no stock is kept by the business.

Lead time: the time it takes for new stock to arrive once it has been ordered.

Legislation: laws set by governments that set out a strict set of rules in which businesses can operate and individuals can act.

Level of output: the number of goods or services being produced by an organisation.

Liability: the legal responsibility that a business owner has to pay the debts of the business.

Line managers: workers in charge of staff during their shift; they are normally paid a higher salary for this responsibility.

Limited liability: when a business cannot pay its debts, the owners (shareholders) are not liable for the debts of the business. All they will lose is the value of their shares, which they have already paid for.

Loan/loan capital: a cash lump sum borrowed (often from a bank) that the business pays back in regular monthly repayments, with interest added.

Local community: a group of people who live and/or work in a geographical area in which a business operates.

Logistics: management of stock in terms of storage and when being transported.

Long-term sources of finance: borrowing for larger amounts of money that can be repaid over longer periods of time (usually longer than 12 months).

Loss: when outgoings (costs) are higher than revenue (income).

M-commerce: transactions made through smartphones.

Managers: individuals who are in charge of a certain group of tasks or group of people.

Manufacturer: a person or business that makes goods.

Margin of safety: the difference between the break-even point and the actual level of sales, i.e. output on top of break-even point.

Market conditions: the characteristics of a market, such as how competitive it is and its growth rate.

Market data: information that relates to a variety of investment markets.

Marketing data: data that helps a business make decisions based on primary and secondary research.

Market map: a diagram used to position and compare products in a market.

Market research: the process of gaining information about customers, competitors and market trends through collecting primary and secondary data.

Market segment: a part of a market that contains a group of buyers with similar buying habits, such as age or income.

Market segmentation: breaking down a market into smaller groups, which are called segments.

Marketing mix: a combination of factors that help a business to take into account customer needs when selling a product, usually summarised as the 4 Ps – price, place, product, promotion.

Market share: the percentage of sales held by a business in a particular market.

Market trends: anything that alters the market that a business operates in.

Maturity phase: the second phase of the product life cycle; sales of the product peak.

Maximum stock level: the highest amount of stock to be kept by a business.

Merger: when two businesses join together.

Minimum stock level (buffer stock): the minimum amount of stock held by a business.

Motivation: when members of staff want to give their best effort and care about the business they work for.

Multinational companies (MNCs): businesses that operate and trade in more than one country.

Net profit: the difference between the amount of money received from selling goods and services and all of the costs incurred to make or provide them; the formula for net profit is: gross profit – other operating expenses and interest.

Net profit margin: the proportion of sales revenue that is left once all costs have been paid; the formula for net profit margin is: net profit ÷ sales revenue × 100.

Objectives: short-term steps taken by an organisation to help it achieve a long-term aim.

Observation: when an employee watches another member of staff to learn how a job is done; also known as shadowing.

One-off costs: costs that a business has to pay for only once, e.g. buying machinery.

Ongoing training: when staff continue to receive training on a regular basis.

Opening balance: the amount of money a business has in its account at the beginning of an accounting period, e.g. a month, a financial year.

Operational staff: staff hired to look after other day-to-day jobs such as receptionists and administration staff.

Order quantity: the amount or quantity of materials ordered.

Organic growth: when a business grows on its own without merging with or taking over any other business; also known as internal growth.

Organisational structure: a diagram showing the internal structure of a business and the roles and responsibilities of the staff who work for it, displayed in levels of authority.

Overdraft: borrowing money from a bank by drawing more money than is actually in a current account, i.e. spending all of the business's money then dipping into the bank's money. Interest is charged by the bank on the amount overdrawn.

Owners: the people that a business belongs to.

Part-time: with regard to employment, staff who gain the same benefits as full-time staff but work for less than 35 hours per week.

Partnership: between 2 and 20 people who own a business and have unlimited liability.

Payment systems: the electronic ability to transfer money quickly and safely from one bank account to another.

Performance reviews: when a member of staff meets with their manager to review their work performance.

Permanent contracts: a contract on an ongoing basis or on an until-further-notice basis.

Person specification: a document prepared by a business that explains what it is seeking in any applicant for a job.

Personal satisfaction: an individual's sense of fulfilment of a need or want.

Personal savings: money that belongs to the owner of a business, for personal use.

Piece rate: a method of paying staff according to how many pieces of work they produce/complete.

Place: a location where customers can purchase goods and services.

Post-sales service: the procedures that a business has in place to support customers after the sale of a good or service.

Pressure groups: groups of people who want to ensure businesses and governments act ethically in relation to the environment/animal welfare/human rights.

Price: the amount that customers have to pay for a product.

Pricing strategy: the plan for setting a product's price.

Primary research: the gathering of new information, called primary data, which has not been collected before; also called field research.

Primary sector: companies and people working to extract raw materials from the earth or the sea.

Private limited company (Ltd): a type of privately held small business. This type of business entity limits owner liability to their shares, limits the number of shareholders to 50, and restricts shareholders from publicly trading the company's shares.

Procurement: the act of obtaining or buying raw materials, components or services from a supplier to be used in the production of goods and services.

Product: term used to describe goods or services.

Product differentiation: making one product different from another in some way, for instance through the quality of its design, packaging or advertising.

Product life cycle: the stages through which a product passes from its development to being withdrawn from sale. The phases are: research and development; launching the product; growth; maturity; saturation; decline.

Product range: a group of similar products made by a business, such as a number of different chocolate bars.

Product trial: used to get customers to try a product for the first time, usually before a business decides to launch it fully to the market.

Production costs: the costs associated with producing goods and services.

Production process: transforming raw materials or inputs into finished products.

Productivity: measures output per worker (or machine) over a period of time.

Profit: where the revenues of a business are greater than its costs over a period of time. Profit = selling price – total costs.

Profitability: how good a business is at making a profit, not simply how much profit it has made.

Promotion (of employee): when an employee rises up the hierarchy of an organisation.

Promotion strategy: a plan to identify the most appropriate promotion methods for a good or service.

Public limited company (plc): a company whose shares can be bought and sold on the stock market.

Qualitative data: information about opinions, judgements and attitudes.

Quality: achieving a minimum standard for a product or service, or a production process, which meets customer needs.

Quality assurance: ensuring that quality is produced and delivered at every stage of the production process, often through making quality the responsibility of every worker involved.

Quality control: ensuring that a product or service meets minimum standards, often through testing of sample products once they have been made.

Quantitative data: data that can be expressed as numbers and statistically analysed.

Quantitative business data: numerical and statistical data.

Raw materials: basic substances that are used to produce finished goods, intermediate materials or energy; sometimes referred to as commodities.

Re-order level: the amount of stock held by a business at which an order for new stock is placed with suppliers.

Remote working: people working together from different locations, whether from home or even from different countries.

Remuneration: financial payment for an employee for completion of work.

Repeat purchase: when a customer buys a product more than once (they return to buy a product again).

Retailer: a business which specialises in selling goods in small quantities to the consumer.

Retained profit: profits that a business has made from previous years of trading.

Revenue: the amount of money/cash coming into a business from selling products over a period of time.

Rewards: the advantages of a course of action, including benefits to an owner.

Risks: the chances of damage or loss occurring as a result of making a decision.

Sale of assets: when a business sells something physical of value to raise capital, e.g. machinery, vehicles, equipment.

Sales: the amount of products or services that are being sold. Sales can also be another word for revenue or income.

Sales process: the steps a business or individual goes through in order to maximise sales of a good or service.

Sales revenue: how much a business receives in payment from selling goods and services to customers.

Secondary research: the process of gathering secondary data, which is information that has already been gathered such as sales records, governments statistics, newspaper reports, Internet or reports from market research groups. Also known as desk research.

Secondary sector: businesses that transform raw materials into finished goods.

Self-learning: when an employee studies without the presence of a teacher or colleague.

Senior managers: responsible for the day-to-day operations of the business in order for the aims and objectives of the business to be achieved.

Services: non-physical, intangible products, e.g. a taxi journey, a haircut, a TV programme.

Share capital: when a registered company sells shares to raise finance in exchange for a share in profits.

Shareholders: people who have bought shares in a business to receive a share in future profits.

Short-term sources of finance: small amounts of borrowing, which must be repaid within one year.

SMART: stands for: specific, measurable, achievable, realistic and timely. SMART is used for objective setting for a business.

Social commerce: transactions made through social media.

Social media: Internet-based forms of communication, e.g. Twitter, Facebook, Instagram.

Social objectives: providing goods and services that are kind to the environment or benefit a community.

Sole trader: the only owner of a business; they have unlimited liability.

Staff turnover: the percentage of staff who leave a business during a certain period of time.

Stakeholders: any person who has an interest in a business and/or is affected by the activities of a business.

Stakeholder conflict: when different stakeholders disagree on business decisions that affect them.

Stock: materials that a business holds. Some stock can be materials waiting to be used in the production process and some can be finished stock waiting to be delivered to customers.

Stock market flotation: when a business becomes a public limited company (plc) and raises capital by inviting members of the public to buy shares in the business.

Supervisors: individuals who work with staff and have the authority to delegate work, and reward and discipline staff; also known as **team leaders**.

Suppliers: businesses that sell (or supply) products to other businesses.

Support staff: people who carry out specific jobs which help facilitate business success, such as computer (IT) technicians, caretakers and canteen staff.

Survival: an aim for an organisation to be able to simply survive in a competitive environment, especially new businesses. Profit may come later.

Sustainable: to make something last longer.

Takeover: when one large business buys a smaller business.

Target market: a specific group of customers (segment) at which a business aims its products.

Tariffs: a tax added onto the selling price of an imported good so that it makes it more expensive to buy in the UK.

Tax: a percentage of profits, income or revenue imposed by the government and paid to the government.

Tax laws: regulations to ensure that businesses are paying the correct taxes to the government.

Temporary contracts: workers who have no permanent contract of employment with a business and so tend to work only for a short period of time for an employer, e.g. supply teacher.

Tertiary sector: companies or people who provide services.

Total costs: when fixed costs and variable costs are added together.

Trade barriers: when a government deliberately restricts opportunities, efficiency and competition for importers in order to protect their own country's businesses against global competition.

Trade blocs: when certain countries group together and agree to make it easier for the members of their group to market for goods, services, capital and labour by getting rid of all barriers to trade.

Trade credit: when a business receives goods from a supplier now but agrees to pay for the goods at a later date.

Trade-off: a compromise between one thing and another when it is not possible to have both things at the same time.

Trading Standards Authority: a body that checks that businesses adhere to strict rules when selling goods and services in order to protect the public from being sold counterfeits.

Training: the action of teaching a person new skills.

Unemployment: when there are not enough jobs for people who are willing and able to work.

Unique selling points: characteristics of a product that make it different from other similar products being sold in the market, e.g. design, quality or image. Also referred to as USPs.

Unlimited liability: where the owner of a business has a legal obligation to pay all the business's debts. If the owner can't pay these debts, the creditor can take possession of the owner's goods, house, etc. and sell them to cover the debt. The business and the owner are deemed to be one and the same entity.

Variable costs: costs that increase as level of output increases, e.g. raw materials, electricity, temporary worker wages.

Venture capital: when external investors with extensive business experience are willing to invest considerable funds into a business at their own risk.

Viral advertising: getting individuals to spread the message about a product through social media networks such as Facebook or their groups of friends.

Viral marketing: when a business uses social media to encourage the public to share information about its goods and services.

Wages: employees paid on an hourly rate.

Wholesaler: a business that buys in bulk from a manufacturer or other supplier and then sells the stock on in smaller quantities to retailers.

Index

Collins

Edexcel GCSE 9-1
Business

Workbook

Cate Calveley, Stephanie Campbell
and Tony Michaelides

Introduction

Contents

Preparing for the GCSE Exam

Experts have found that there are two techniques that help you to retain and recall information and consistently produce better results in exams compared to other revision techniques. It really isn't rocket science either – you simply need to **test yourself** on each topic as many times as possible and **leave a gap** between the test sessions.

Tip 1. Use Your Time Wisely

- Try to start revising six months before your exams – it's more effective and less stressful.
- Your revision time is precious so use it wisely – using the techniques described on this page will ensure you revise effectively and efficiently and get the best results.
- Don't waste time re-reading the same information over and over again – it's not effective!

Tip 2. Make a Plan

- Identify all the topics you need to revise (this Complete Revision & Practice book will help you).
- Plan at least five sessions for each topic.
- One hour should be ample time to test yourself on the key ideas for a topic.
- Spread out the practice sessions for each topic – the optimum time to leave between each session is about one month but, if this isn't possible, just make the gaps as big as you can.

Tip 3. Test Yourself

- Methods for testing yourself include: quizzes, practice questions, flashcards, past papers, explaining a topic to someone else, etc.
- This Complete Revision & Practice book provides seven practice opportunities per topic.
- Don't worry if you get an answer wrong – provided you check what the correct answer is, you are more likely to get the same or a similar question right in future!

Visit **collins.co.uk/collinsGCSErevision** to download your free flashcards and for more information about the benefits of these revision techniques.

Command Verbs

This table gives information about the command verbs that you will find in your exam questions.

Command verb	Meaning	Guidance	Marks available
Select	Choose one or more correct answers from the options. These questions test recall of knowledge from the specification content.		1–2
Define	Define a term from the specification content.	*One point of knowledge*	1
Give	Give an answer testing recall of knowledge from the specification content.	*One point of knowledge*	1
State	State one point of knowledge as detailed in the specification within the context of a given case study.	*One point of knowledge + One example of context embedded in the answer*	2
Identify	Identify the correct answer from reading a graph or table of data.		1
Calculate	Use mathematical skills to reach the answer, based on given data. Calculators may be used, and workings should be given.	*Formula + Figures + Final answer*	2
Complete the table	Work out the values missing from the presented table of data.		2
Outline	Give two linked points about a business concept or issue, placed in context in the question.	*One point of knowledge + One linked strand of relevant development + Context*	2
Explain	Give a statement of fact, with two further expansion points. These may expand on each other or on the same fact. There is no context in these questions.	*One point of knowledge + Two linked strands of relevant development*	3
Discuss	Write an extended answer, requiring expansion and exploration of a business concept or issue. These questions will not have context, but you can bring one in to illustrate your answer.	*One or two points of knowledge + Five linked strands of relevant development across the answer*	6
Analyse	Write an extended answer, requiring expansion and exploration of a business concept or issue. The answer will be placed in context by the question.	*One or two points of knowledge + Five linked strands of relevant development + Context across the answer*	6
Justify	Write an extended answer, using knowledge of specification content to reach a supported conclusion about a business situation.	*Make a judgement with value.* ***Analyse** the reasons for your decision (see structure above).* ***Explain** one point of balance (see structure above) + Context.* *Conclude by **explaining** one new point of knowledge that supports your choice + Context.*	9
Evaluate	Write an extended answer, using knowledge of specification content to reach a supported conclusion about a business situation.	*Make a judgement with value.* ***Analyse** the reasons for your decision (see structure above).* ***Explain** one point of balance (see structure above) + Context.* *Conclude by **explaining** one new point of knowledge that supports your choice + Context.*	12

Adapted from: Pearson Edexcel Level 1/Level 2 GCSE (9–1) in Business – Specification Issue 2 – July 2022

Enterprise and Entrepreneurship

1 Give **one** reason why new business ideas are created.

.... [1]

2 Explain **one** risk that an entrepreneur faces when starting up a new business.

....

....

.... [3]

3 Explain **one** way that changes in consumer tastes can support the introduction of new business ideas.

....

....

.... [3]

4 Explain **one** way that a business can meet customer needs.

....

....

.... [3]

5 Which **one** of the following best describes the term 'added value'?

Select **one** answer.

A An investment to start a business ☐

B Charging a higher price for a product than competitors ☐

C Revenue minus costs ☐

D The difference between the cost of inputs and the price
   that consumers are willing to pay for them ☐ [1]

6 Give **one** role of an entrepreneur.

.... [1]

7 Which **two** of the following are factors of production?

Select **two** answers.

A Capital ☐

B Cash ☐

C Loan ☐

D Labour ☐

E Product ☐ [2]

8 Identify **one** impact of having a unique selling point for a business.

....

.... [1]

9 Explain **one** way that making business decisions contributes to the role of an entrepreneur.

....

....

....

.... [3]

10 Explain **one** reason why entrepreneurial skills are important when starting a business.

....

....

....

.... [3]

11 Which **one** of the following is an example of a change in technology?

Select **one** answer.

A Smart home devices that can control heating temperature ☐

B Charging for plastic bags in supermarkets ☐

C Changes in interest rates ☐

D Business e-commerce ☐ [1]

Spotting a Business Opportunity

1 Give **one** way in which a small business can identify customer needs.

.... [1]

2 Explain **one** advantage to a small business of using social media to collect market research data.

....

....

.... [3]

3 Give **one** drawback of collecting secondary market research.

.... [1]

4 Explain **one** way in which a small business could target customers using market segmentation.

....

....

....

.... [3]

5 Explain **one** advantage to a small business of using quantitative data for market research.

....

....

....

.... [3]

6 Which **two** of the following are examples of qualitative data?

Select **two** answers.

A Memories ☐

B Opinions ☐

C Feelings ☐

D Pictures ☐

E Numbers ☐   [2]

7 Explain **one** way that market mapping allows a small business to spot gaps in the market.

_____

_____

_____ [3]

8 Which **one** of the following helps a small business to gain a competitive advantage?

Select **one** answer.

A High competition ☐   **C** Low costs ☐

B High cash outflow ☐   **D** Low cash inflow ☐ [1]

9 Identify **one** impact of increased competition on a business.

_____

_____ [1]

10 Give **one** method that small businesses use to compete.

_____ [1]

11 Explain **one** advantage to a business of having a prime location.

_____

_____

_____ [3]

12 Explain **one** reason why a small business must price its products at the correct level.

_____

_____

_____ [3]

13 Define the term 'market trends'.

_____ [1]

Putting a Business Idea into Practice

1 Explain **one** limitation of creating a cash-flow forecast.

....

....

....

[3]

2 The table below shows information about a business.

	January	February
Cash inflow	£25 000	£25 000
Cash outflow	£20 000	£21 000
Net cash-flow	£5 000	£4 000
Opening balance	£4 000	
Closing balance		£13 000

Using the information above, calculate the closing balance for January and the opening balance for February.

You are advised to show your workings.

....

....

[2]

3 The tables below show information about a business.

Fixed cost	£250 000
Selling price	£125

Variable cost per unit	£25
Quantity	10 000

a) Using the information given, calculate the break-even point for the business.

You are advised to show your workings.

....

....

[2]

b) Using the information given, calculate the margin of safety.

You are advised to show your workings.

....

....

[2]

4 Explain **one** disadvantage of using an overdraft as a source of finance.

[3]

5 Explain **one** impact of the rise in variable costs on the break-even level of output.

[3]

6 The table below shows information relating to a business loan.

Amount borrowed	£50 000
Amount repaid	£55 000

Using the information above, calculate the percentage interest rate.

You are advised to show your workings.

[2]

7 The table below shows information relating to a business loan.

Amount borrowed	£70 000
Amount repaid	£85 000

Using the information above, calculate the percentage interest rate.

You are advised to show your workings.

[2]

Making the Business Effective

1 Which **one** of the following best describes a **shareholder**?

Select **one** answer.

A   A person who is the sole owner of a business ☐

B   A person who owns a share of a business ☐

C   A person who owns a business with one or more other people ☐

D   A person who started a business with one or more other people ☐   [1]

2 Give the name of the tax that is paid by **limited companies**.

_____   [1]

3 Give **one** factor that may influence the location of a business.

_____   [1]

4 Identify **one** impact of being a sole trader on a small business.

_____

_____   [1]

5 Which **one** of the following is a characteristic of a partnership?

Select **one** answer.

A   Can sell shares to anyone ☐

B   There is one single owner ☐

C   There are between 2 and 20 owners ☐

D   Shareholders start the business ☐   [1]

6 Explain **one** benefit to an entrepreneur of starting a business as a franchise.

_____

_____

_____   [3]

7 Define the term 'e-commerce'.

_____   [1]

8 Explain **one** disadvantage to a business of locating close to competitors.

[3]

9 Which **one** of the following best describes the product element of the marketing mix?
Select **one** answer.

A   How the product will reach the customer ☐

B   The way a business will encourage customers to make a purchase ☐

C   A good or service being offered by a business ☐

D   The amount customers pay for a good or service ☐ [1]

10 Explain **one** disadvantage to a business of using digital communication as a way of informing customers about special offers.

[3]

11 Identify **one** benefit to a business of having a balanced marketing mix.

[1]

12 Explain **one** reason why it is important to include financial information in a business plan.

[3]

13 Identify **one** way a business plan could help a small start-up business.

[1]

Understanding External Influences on Business

1 Explain **one** impact a supplier might have on a business.

....

....

....

[3]

2 Explain **one** way in which a pressure group could impact a business.

....

....

....

[3]

3 Give **two** examples of digital communication.

....

....

[2]

4 Explain **one** impact a consumer can have on a business.

....

....

....

[3]

5 Which **one** of the following refers to the stakeholder that provides a business with raw materials?
Select **one** answer.

A Supplier ☐   **C** Shareholder ☐

B Customer ☐   **D** Competitor ☐   [1]

6 Which **one** of the following refers to the stakeholder that purchases goods and services from a business?
Select **one** answer.

A Supplier ☐   **C** Shareholder ☐

B Customer ☐   **D** Competitor ☐   [1]

7 Which **one** of the following refers to the stakeholder that owns a business?
Select **one** answer.

A Supplier ☐   **C** Shareholder ☐

B Customer ☐   **D** Competitor ☐   [1]

8 Explain **one** disadvantage of digital communication to a business.

_____

_____

_____   [3]

9 Explain **one** way in which digital communication impacts the marketing mix.

_____

_____

_____   [3]

10 Explain **one** way in which employment legislation impacts a business.

_____

_____

_____   [3]

11 A business purchases $15 000 worth of imports at an exchange rate of £1 = $1.35

Calculate the amount that the imports cost in £. You are advised to show your workings.

_____

_____   [2]

12 A business sells £20 000 worth of exports at an exchange rate of £1 = $1.25

Calculate the value of exports in $. You are advised to show your workings.

_____

_____   [2]

Growing the Business

1 Explain **one** limitation of a public limited company.

[3]

2 Explain **one** advantage of selling assets.

[3]

3 Explain **one** reason how market conditions could impact the aims and objectives of a business.

[3]

4 Explain **one** reason why imports to the UK might increase.

[3]

5 Explain **one** reason why exports from the UK might increase.

[3]

6 Explain **one** reason how selling in a foreign country might impact the marketing mix.

_____

_____

_____ [3]

7 Which **one** of the following is an internal source of finance?
Select **one** answer.

A Selling assets ☐   **C** Venture capital ☐

B Share capital ☐   **D** Loan ☐ [1]

8 Which **one** of the following describes a business that sells in more than one country?
Select **one** answer.

A Sole trader ☐   **C** Private limited company ☐

B Partnership ☐   **D** Multinational corporation ☐ [1]

9 Give **one** objective of a customer.

_____ [1]

10 Give **one** example of a trading bloc.

_____ [1]

11 Explain **one** reason why a business might use share capital as a source of finance.

_____

_____

_____ [3]

Making Marketing Decisions

1 Identify **one** benefit to a business of withdrawing a product that has entered the decline phase of its life cycle.

....

.... [1]

2 Give **one** strategy a business could use to extend the life cycle of a product.

.... [1]

3 Explain **one** method a business could use to differentiate a product.

....

....

....

.... [3]

4 Identify **one** drawback to a business of using sponsorship as a method of promoting its products.

....

.... [1]

5 Define the term 'profit margin'.

....

.... [1]

6 Explain **one** disadvantage to a business of using a low margin, high volume pricing strategy.

....

....

....

.... [3]

7 Which **two** of the following are examples of pricing strategies?

Select **two** answers.

A Cost plus ☐

B Skimming ☐

C Functionality ☐

D E-commerce ☐

E Contribution ☐ [2]

8 Which **one** of the following is a method of promotion for a business?

Select **one** answer.

A Retailer ☐   **C** Special offers ☐

B Skimming ☐   **D** E-commerce ☐ [1]

9 Explain **one** benefit to a business of using social media to promote its products.

_____

_____

_____ [3]

10 Which **one** of the following is a distribution method for a business?

Select **one** answer.

A Location ☐   **C** Resources ☐

B E-tailer ☐   **D** Manufacturing ☐ [1]

11 Explain **one** benefit to a business of having an integrated marketing mix.

_____

_____

_____ [3]

Making Operational Decisions

1 Explain **one** disadvantage to a business of using batch production.

[3]

2 Identify **one** impact technology has had on production.

[1]

3 Define the term 'economies of scale'.

[1]

4 The diagram shows the bar gate stock graph for deliveries of a business in the month of January. There are two deliveries, marked A and B.

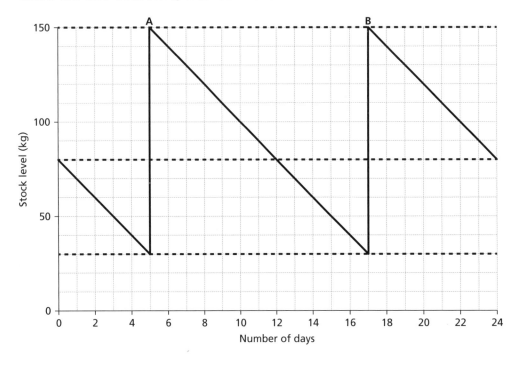

a) Identify the reorder level in kilograms for the business in the month of January.

[1]

b) Identify how many days it takes for the business to receive delivery A.

[1]

5 Which **one** of the following best describes **quality assurance**?

Select **one** answer.

A   Quality is part of the production process; at every stage quality is checked
by workers ☐

B   Quality is checked at the end of the production process ☐

C   Quality is checked only at the beginning of the production process ☐

D   Quality is checked at the beginning and end of the production process ☐ [1]

6 Which **two** of the following are factors to consider when choosing a supplier?

Select **two** answers.

A   Local elections ☐

B   Post offices ☐

C   Availability ☐

D   Trust ☐

E   Advertising ☐ [2]

7 Explain **one** benefit to a business of responding to negative feedback.

_____

_____

_____ [3]

1 Explain **one** way in which a business can increase its net profit.

[3]

2 Give **two** examples of a variable cost.

[2]

3 The table below shows the financial records of a business.

Total revenue	£360 000
Cost of sales	£190 000
Gross profit	£170 000
Overheads	£85 000

Using the information above, calculate the gross profit margin of the business.
You are advised to show your workings.

[2]

4 The table below shows the financial records of a business.

Total revenue	£550 000
Cost of sales	
Gross profit	£150 000
Overheads	£100 000
Net profit	

Using the information above, calculate the cost of sales and net profit of the business.
You are advised to show your workings.

[2]

5 The table below shows information about a business.

Sales revenue	£200 000
Gross profit	£30 000
Expenses	£10 000

a) Using the information above, calculate the gross profit margin of the business.
You are advised to show your workings.

[2]

b) Using the information above, calculate the net profit margin of the business.
You are advised to show your workings.

[2]

6 The table below shows information about a business.

Average annual profit	£45 000
Initial investment	£400 000

Using the information in the table, calculate the average rate of return for this investment.
You are advised to show your workings.

[2]

7 Explain **one** reason why a business records gross profit.

[3]

Making Human Resource Decisions

1 Which **one** of the following is a financial method of motivation?
Select **one** answer.

A Job rotation ☐   **C** Job enlargement ☐

B Fringe benefits ☐   **D** Autonomy ☐   [1]

2 Which **one** of the following is a benefit of training staff?
Select **one** answer.

A Increased productivity ☐   **C** Increased absenteeism ☐

B Increased labour turnover ☐   **D** Decrease in skills ☐   [1]

3 Explain **one** purpose of a candidate filling out an application form.

[3]

4 Explain **one** disadvantage of flexible working to a business.

[3]

5 Explain **one** benefit of part-time working to a business.

[3]

6 Explain **one** limitation of job enlargement on a business.

[3]

7 Explain **one** benefit of external recruitment to a business.

[3]

8 Identify **one** method of training.

[1]

9 Explain **one** purpose of induction training for a business.

[3]

10 Explain **one** limitation of training on a business.

[3]

11 Explain **one** reason why a business conducts performance reviews of its employees.

[3]

12 Explain **one** impact of excessive communication.

[3]

THIS PAGE HAS DELIBERATELY BEEN LEFT BLANK

Collins

GCSE 9–1 Edexcel Business
Paper 1: Investigating small business

Time: 1 hour 45 minutes

Instructions

- Use **black** ink or black ball-point pen.
- **Fill in the boxes** at the bottom of this page.
- There are **three** sections in this paper.
- Answer **all** questions. You must answer the questions in the spaces provided.
- Calculators may be used.
- You are advised to **show all your working out** with **your answer clearly shown** at **the end**.

Information

- The total mark for this paper is 90.
- The marks for **each** question are shown in brackets – **use this as a guide as to how much time you should spend on each question**.

Advice

- You must read the questions provided with care before attempting to answer.
- Make every attempt to answer all questions provided.
- If you have time, check your answers.

Candidate surname:	Other names:

* Note that in your actual exam, the business case studies will be contained within a separate Source Booklet.

Section A

Answer ALL questions.
Write your answers in the spaces provided.

Some questions must be answered with a cross in a box ☒. If you change your mind about an answer, put a line through the box ☒ and then mark your new answer with a cross ☒.

---

1   (a)   Which **one** of the following is **not** an element of the marketing mix?

Select **one** answer.   (1)

☐   **A**   Price

☐   **B**   Product

☐   **C**   Procurement

☐   **D**   Promotion

(b)   Which **one** of the following is **not** a method of secondary research?

Select **one** answer.   (1)

☐   **A**   The Internet

☐   **B**   Statistics

☐   **C**   Surveys

☐   **D**   Market reports

(c)   Explain **one** reason why access to cash is important to a small business.   (3)

....

....

....

....

....

....

(d) Explain **one** drawback of e-commerce to a business. (3)

....

....

....

....

....

....

(Total for Question 1 = 8 marks)

2 **(a)** Which **two** of the following are examples of short-term finance?

Select **two** answers. (2)

☐ **A** Overdraft

☐ **B** Venture capital

☐ **C** Loan

☐ **D** Trade credit

☐ **E** Mortgage

(b) Which **two** of the following are examples of a financial aim?

Select **two** answers. (2)

☐ **A** Survival

☐ **B** Market share

☐ **C** Independence and control

☐ **D** Challenge

☐ **E** Personal satisfaction

The table below shows the cash-flow forecast for a small business.

(c) Complete the table with the **two** missing figures. (2)

	September (£)	October (£)
Cash inflows	(i) _____	24 000
Cash outflows	18 200	16 500
Net cash-flow	8 600	7 500
Opening balance	10 000	18 600
Closing balance	18 600	(ii) _____

(d) Explain **one** disadvantage of health and safety legislation to a small business. (3)

(e) Explain **one** advantage of operating as a sole trader. (3)

(Total for Question 2 = 12 marks)

3 **(a)** Which **one** of the following is **not** a role of business enterprise?

Select **one** answer. **(1)**

◻ **A** Produce goods and services

◻ **B** Make a profit

◻ **C** Meet customer needs

◻ **D** Add value

The figure below shows information about the financial performance of a business from April to June.

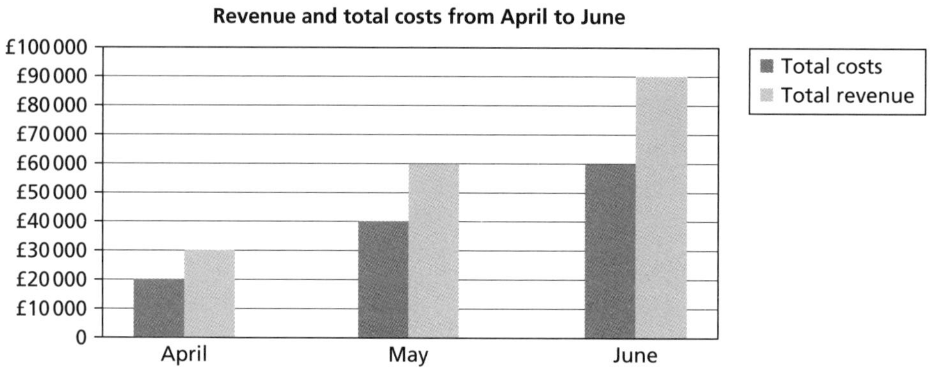

Revenue and total costs from April to June

(b) Using the information in the figure above, calculate the total profit for the period April to June.

You are advised to show your workings. **(2)**

£ ....

(c) Explain **one** advantage to a small business of using trade credit as a source of finance. **(3)**

....

....

....

....

....

....

(d) Explain **one** disadvantage of using focus groups as a method of market research. **(3)**

(e) Discuss the impact of high unemployment on a small business. **(6)**

(Total for Question 3 = 15 marks)

TOTAL FOR SECTION A = 35 MARKS

Practice Exam Paper 1

Section B

Answer ALL questions.
Write your answers in the spaces provided.

Read the following extract before answering Questions 4, 5 and 6.

Opened in 2018, The Hare on the Hill is a gastro restaurant in Littleborough, a small village in the foothills of the Pennines. It has an excellent reputation for quality food and outstanding service, delivered by Adam and his team, that keeps those in the know coming back over and over again.

As well as an indoor dining space with cosy seatings areas and an open fire, it has custom-built garden chalets, each individually styled and complete with adjustable heating, Wi-Fi and music.

The Hare on the Hill has a varied menu and the staff pride themselves on creating incredible grazing platters packed with a variety of fresh meats and cheeses, all with a distinctly British feel and wherever possible using local ingredients to make sure everything they do "is just that little bit better".

(Source: adapted from https://beerbreadpork.pub/)

4 **(a)** Outline **one** possible non-financial aim The Hare on the Hill may have had when starting as a small business. (2)

....

....

....

....

(b) Analyse the importance of the product element in The Hare on the Hill's market mix. (6)

....

....

....

....

....

....

....

....

....

....

....

....

(Total for Question 4 = 8 marks)

5 The Hare on the Hill has the following financial information for the month of June.

	June
Raw materials for each platter	£12.50
Fixed costs	£2730.00
Selling price for each platter	£21.00
Total revenue	£7980.00

(a) Using the information in the table above, calculate the number of platters sold in June.

You are advised to show your workings. (2)

.... platters

(b) Using the information in the table above, calculate the profit The Hare on the Hill is forecast to make from selling platters in June.

You are advised to show your workings. (2)

£ ....

(c) Analyse the importance to The Hare on the Hill of complying with health and safety legislation.

(6)

....

....

....

....

....

....

....

....

....

....

....

....

(Total for Question 5 = 10 marks)

6 **(a)** State **one** example of a fixed cost The Hare on the Hill would have to pay. (1)

(b) Outline **one** method of primary market research that The Hare on the Hill could use to research its customers' wants and needs. (2)

(c) In order to improve profits, The Hare on the Hill is considering two options:

Option 1: Use targeted advertising on social media.

Option 2: Increase the selling prices of its platters.

Justify which **one** of these two options The Hare on the Hill should choose. (9)

(Total for Question 6 = 12 marks)

TOTAL FOR SECTION B = 30 MARKS

Section C

Answer ALL questions.
Write your answers in the spaces provided.

Read the following extract before answering Question 7.

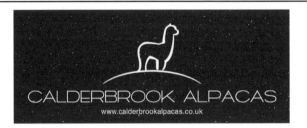

Calderbrook Alpacas was founded in 2018 by sole trader Joanne for one main reason... to make people smile! Customer satisfaction is Joanne's most important aim.

Joanne operates as a tourist attraction selling walks and meet-and-greet experiences. Customers come to spend a morning or afternoon with her 14 alpacas and one sheep. Joanne's customer base is mainly made up of families with children looking for an outdoor activity. However, she also takes her baby alpacas to schools for animal education days, to care homes for therapeutic experiences and to businesses promoting staff wellbeing. Therefore, customers who cannot travel to her site are still able to enjoy the animals.

Joanne would like to expand her operations to increase the size of her herd to be able to offer experiences to multiple groups of customers at a time. She is currently considering her options for growth.

Calderbrook Alpacas is managed on a day-to-day basis with the help of digital technology. Joanne has a presence on all social media platforms as well as a website. Customers can book with her via WhatsApp, on her website or by telephone. Her social media accounts are updated weekly with highlights from all experiences that have been attended. She runs competitions to ask her followers to guess the alpaca from photographs she has taken and promotes up-and-coming booking opportunities. Joanne also includes a 'Buy Now' button on all her social media posts.

(Source: adapted from https://calderbrookalpacas.co.uk)

7 **(a)** State **one** market segment Calderbrook Alpacas might target. (1)

....

....

(b) The figure below shows customer insight information generated from followers of the Facebook page of Calderbrook Alpacas.

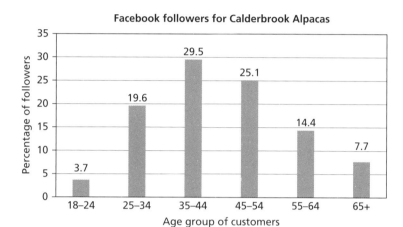

Facebook followers for Calderbrook Alpacas

Using the information in the figure above, identify what percentage of customers are aged 45 and over.

You are advised to show your workings. (1)

.... %

(c) Outline **one** way in which a business plan could reduce the risk of failure of Calderbrook Alpacas. (2)

....

....

....

....

(d) Joanne is looking to add four more alpacas to her herd. Each alpaca could cost around £1 200. In order to expand, Calderbrook Alpacas is considering two finance options:

Option 1: Retained profit

Option 2: Loan capital

Justify which **one** of these two options Calderbrook Alpacas should choose. (9)

(e) Evaluate the extent to which social media helps Calderbrook Alpacas achieve its main non-financial aim of customer enjoyment and satisfaction.

You should use the information you are provided with as well as your knowledge of business. **(12)**

(Total for Question 7 = 25 marks)
TOTAL FOR SECTION C = 25 MARKS
TOTAL FOR PAPER = 90 MARKS

THIS PAGE HAS DELIBERATELY BEEN LEFT BLANK

Collins

GCSE 9–1 Edexcel Business
Paper 2: Building a business

Time: 1 hour 45 minutes

Instructions

- Use **black** ink or black ball-point pen.
- **Fill in the boxes** at the bottom of this page.
- There are **three** sections in this paper.
- Answer **all** questions. You must answer the questions in the spaces provided.
- Calculators may be used.
- You are advised to **show all your working** with **your answer clearly shown** at **the end**.

Information

- The maximum mark for this paper is 90.
- The marks for **each** question are shown in brackets – **use this as a guide as to how much time you should spend on each question.**

Advice

- You must read the questions provided with care before attempting to answer.
- Make every attempt to answer all questions provided.
- If you have time, check your answers.

Candidate surname:	Other names:

* Note that in your actual exam, the business case studies will be contained within a separate Source Booklet.

Practice Exam Paper 2

Section A

Answer ALL questions.
Write your answers in the spaces provided.

Some questions must be answered with a cross in a box ☒. If you change your mind about an answer, put a line through the box ☒ and then mark your new answer with a cross ☒.

---

1 **(a)** Which **one** of the following is **not** a method of organic growth?

Select **one** answer. (1)

☐ **A** Innovation

☐ **B** Merger

☐ **C** Research and development

☐ **D** Opening additional branches

(b) Which **one** of the following is a barrier to international trade?

Select **one** answer. (1)

☐ **A** Import

☐ **B** Export

☐ **C** Tariff

☐ **D** Multinational

(c) Explain **one** benefit to a business of using the Bar Gate Stock Control method. (3)

....

....

....

....

....

....

....

(d) Explain **one** drawback for a business of off-the-job training. (3)

....

....

....

....

....

....

(Total for Question 1 = 8 marks)

2 **(a)** Which **two** of the following are examples of financial motivation?

Select **two** answers. (2)

◻ **A** Remuneration

◻ **B** Job rotation

◻ **C** Autonomy

◻ **D** Commission

◻ **E** Job enrichment

(b) Which **two** of the following are elements of the sales process?

Select **two** answers. (2)

◻ **A** Logistics

◻ **B** Trust

◻ **C** Availability

◻ **D** Speed and efficiency

◻ **E** Product knowledge

The table below contains information about a new machine that a business wants to purchase.

Average annual profit	£300 000
Cost of new machine	£600 000

(c) Using the information in the table above, calculate the average rate of return from the investment.

You are advised to show your workings. (2)

....%

(d) Explain **one** advantage of a decentralised organisational structure. (3)

_____

_____

_____

_____

_____

(e) Explain **one** advantage of flow production. (3)

_____

_____

_____

_____

_____

(Total for Question 2 = 12 marks)

3 **(a)** Which **one** of the following is **not** an external source of finance?

Select **one** answer. (1)

- [ ] **A** Selling assets
- [ ] **B** Loan capital
- [ ] **C** Stock market flotation
- [ ] **D** Share capital

The table below shows information about a business.

Sales revenue	£50 000
Gross profit	£10 000
Other operating expenses and interest	£25 000

(b) Using the information in the table above, calculate the gross profit margin for the first quarter of the year.

You are advised to show your workings. (2)

.... %

(c) Explain **one** advantage of using gross profit margin as a performance measure. (3)

(d) Explain **one** way in which an integrated market mix can influence competitive advantage.

(3)

(e) Discuss the importance of product differentiation to a business. (6)

(Total for Question 3 = 15 marks)
TOTAL FOR SECTION A = 35 MARKS

Section B

Answer ALL questions.
Write your answers in the spaces provided.

Read the following extract before answering Questions 4, 5 and 6.

TALARIA UK

Talaria UK is the largest distributor of Talaria E-Bikes in the UK. With a growing network of carefully selected dealers, it offers extensive support for sales, servicing and parts back-up. Talaria dirt bikes are developed and manufactured in Chongqing, China. Since launching in late 2021 with the off-road *Sting*, the Talaria UK brand has gone from strength to strength and has now become a highly sought-after machine in the electric motorcycle market.

Talaria has now launched the latest product in its range, the *Sting R* which boasts an all-new air-cooled motor with a nominal power of 4 kW and a peak of 8 kW – a 33% increase from the original *Sting*. With an 18% increase in the battery size from 38 Ah to 45 Ah, the *Sting R* has notably faster acceleration and a 13% increase in top speed. The new 2.7 kW battery also brings an increased range of 53 miles. Finally, charging time has reduced by 25%, charging from 0–100% in just 3 hours.

This wealth of innovative developments makes the *Sting R* an industry leader in a marketplace that is already populated with strong brand competitors like Honda and Yamaha, and it is potentially the bike of choice for up-and-coming championship riders like young brothers Bruce and Malachy Tetley.

(Source: adapted from https://www.talariauk.com)

4 **(a)** Outline **one** influence on Talaria's pricing strategy. (2)

....

....

....

....

(b) Analyse the importance of function in Talaria's design mix. (6)

....

....

....

....

....

....

....

....

....

(Total for Question 4 = 8 marks)

5 The table below contains information about the price of two *Sting* models sold by Talaria.

	Price
Sting R (Standard)	£4 595
Sting R (Expert)	£5 395

(a) Using the information in the table above, calculate to 2 decimal places the percentage increase in the price of the *Expert* model compared to the *Standard* model.

You are advised to show your workings. (2)

.... %

(b) Using the information in the table above, calculate the average price of a Talaria *Sting R* bike.

You are advised to show your workings. (2)

£ ....

(c) Analyse the importance to Talaria of research and development. (6)

....

....

....

....

....

....

....

....

....

....

(Total for Question 5 = 10 marks)

6 **(a)** State **one** method of distribution Talaria could use. (1)

....

....

(b) Outline **one** impact of Talaria using external sources of finance to invest in the
research and development of its product range. (2)

....

....

....

....

(c) In order to improve the promotion element of its market mix, Talaria is considering two options:

Option 1: Sponsorship

Option 2: Viral advertising

Justify which **one** of these two options you think Talaria should choose. (9)

(Total for Question 6 = 12 marks)

TOTAL FOR SECTION B = 30 MARKS

Section C

Answer ALL questions.
Write your answers in the spaces provided.

Read the following extract before answering Question 7.

Dubrovnik Weddings is a company that provides a wedding planning service. It started as a small company with one employee whose mission was to create bespoke and unforgettable wedding experiences in Croatia.

Over the last few years, Dubrovnik Weddings has expanded the services that it offers for both corporate and private events. The company now provides wedding planning services to clients from all over the world.

Croatia has seen a massive increase in tourism over the last 10 years and this has in turn led to people wanting to get married there.

Dubrovnik Weddings expanded its workforce by employing overseas wedding planners as it felt this would give the client a better experience and customer service.

With the rise in social media, Dubrovnik Weddings had to move quickly to keep up with the trends as it felt that the use of social media and digital marketing was vital for its growth.

Employees of Dubrovnik Weddings regularly visit local venues and build up strong relationships with suppliers in order to get the best rates. They source produce that can be quickly delivered to the weddings, which has the additional benefit of supporting local businesses.

(Source: adapted from interview with Claire Geraghty, UK Consultant, Dubrovnik Weddings)

7   (a)   State **one** service Dubrovnik Weddings may offer to clients.   (1)

....

....

The figure below shows customer insight information on where the clients of Dubrovnik Weddings come from.

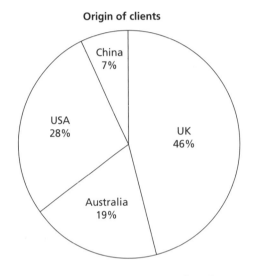

Origin of clients

(b)   Using the information in the figure above, identify what percentage of customers represent sales from the UK and the USA.

You are advised to show your workings.   (1)

.... %

(c)   Outline **one** impact on Dubrovnik Weddings of recruiting wedding planners from many different countries.   (2)

....

....

....

....

(d) High levels of motivation are essential to ensure employees are giving customers the best service possible. To ensure that its staff are highly motivated, Dubrovnik Weddings is considering two options:

Option 1: Financial motivation

Option 2: Non-financial motivation

Justify which **one** of these two options Dubrovnik Weddings should choose.　　(9)

(e) Evaluate the importance to Dubrovnik Weddings of providing excellent customer service.

You should use the information you are provided with as well as your knowledge of business.

(12)

(Total for Question 7 = 25 marks)

TOTAL FOR SECTION C = 25 MARKS

TOTAL FOR PAPER = 90 MARKS

Answers

1. **Any one from:** old products become obsolete; accidental discovery; innovation; invention [1]
2. **Possible answer:** An entrepreneur faces financial risk [1] because a financial investment is required to start a new business [1]. Therefore, there is a risk that the entrepreneur may lose this money if the business fails [1].
3. **Possible answer:** Changes in consumer tastes can increase the popularity of products [1]. If demand for a product is high in a market, businesses will respond by making more of these products [1]. This gives an opportunity for new businesses to break into the market to continue to meet consumer demand [1].
4. **Possible answer:** A business can meet customer needs by being convenient [1]. If the business makes the product easily available to buy when the customer needs it [1], there may be more sales [1].
5. D [1]
6. **Any one from:** organise resources; make decisions; take risks [1]
7. A [1]; D [1]
8. Products will be differentiated from others in the same market. [1]
9. **Possible answer:** An entrepreneur must make decisions to effectively manage the resources of the business [1]. Handling resources effectively and assessing opportunities will help the business to meet customer needs [1] and therefore become successful [1].
10. **Possible answer:** Entrepreneurial skills are important as there are many challenges an entrepreneur faces [1] when starting a business. They will need to have a range of skills that work together to help the business be successful [1]. If the correct risks are not taken, opportunities can be missed and the business can fail [1].
11. A [1]

1. Market research [1]
2. **Possible answer:** The data is cheap or free to obtain [1] and it gives the business information about how it can put more money into improving or adapting a product [1]. This will lead to satisfied customers and more sales [1].
3. It can be out of date. [1]
4. **Possible answer:** A small business could segment its market using income [1]. Those that earn a high level of income may be more attracted to premium or luxury products that cost more money [1]. A business may therefore introduce a product that is high quality to meet that customer demand [1].
5. **Possible answer:** The data is numerical [1] and can therefore be measured easily [1]. This means that it will be easier for a small business to make a judgement on customer preferences [1].
6. B [1]; C [1]
7. **Possible answer:** Mapping out all the businesses in the market makes it easier to identify opportunities [1]. This can help a small business to develop products to fill the gaps, provided they are profitable [1]. This will help the business to grow its market share [1].
8. C [1]
9. A business will need to reconsider its pricing strategy if there are many competitors in the same market. [1]
10. **Any one from:** price; quality; location; product range; customer service [1]
11. Having a prime location will mean the business is accessible to its customers [1]. This will meet its customers' needs [1] and lead to more sales and revenue for the business [1].
12. **Possible answer:** The price affects the perceived quality of the product [1]. Customers will try to get the best quality for the most reasonable price [1]. Therefore, it is important that a small business prices its product at the right level for the quality that customers expect [1].
13. Anything that alters the market that a business operates in [1]

1. **Possible answer:** A limitation of a cash-flow forecast is that it may not be accurate [1]. It is impossible to predict the future and therefore the figures created might not be accurate owing to external factors, such as a recession [1]. This means the business may act on inaccurate information, leading to poor decision making [1].
2. Closing balance for January = £5000 + £4000 = £9000 [1]
   Opening balance for February = £9000 [1]
3. a) $\dfrac{£250\,000}{(£125 - £25)}$ [1] = 2500 [1]

   b) 10000 − 2500 [1] = 7500 [1]
4. **Possible answer:** A disadvantage of using an overdraft is that you are only able to borrow a limited amount of money from the bank [1]. This may not be sufficient to pay for day-to-day expenses for the business [1]. This means the business may need to look for an alternative source of finance [1].
5. **Possible answer:** A rise in variable cost will mean that the business has to sell more goods and services in order to break even [1]. This is because the contribution per unit is smaller so it will need to sell more units [1] to repay the fixed costs [1].
6. £55000 − £50000 = £5000
   $\dfrac{£5000}{£50000} \times 100$ [1] = 10% [1]
7. £85000 − £70000 = £15000
   $\dfrac{£15000}{£70000} \times 100$ [1] = 21.43% [1]

1. B [1]
2. Corporation tax [1]
3. **Any one from:** nature of the business; proximity to market; labour; materials; competitors [1]
4. The owner is their own boss and can make all the business decisions. [1]
5. C [1]
6. **Possible answer:** A franchise has an established brand that already exists [1]. This means that customers will already know and be attracted to its products [1], so the risk of setting up the franchise is much lower than creating a new business idea [1].
7. The ability to buy and sell products over the Internet [1]
8. **Possible answer:** It gives customers more choice [1]. The business may attract customers who then decide to buy from a competitor located close by [1]. This can lead to a loss of market share [1].
9. C [1]
10. **Possible answer:** Digital communication can be missed by customers or be left unopened [1]. This leads to low response rates [1]. As a result, not all customers will be informed about the special offers, leading to a loss of potential sales [1].
11. Balancing product, price, promotion and place will ensure that a business is meeting customers' needs. [1]
12. **Possible answer:** It helps the business to borrow money from banks and lenders [1] and prove that it can be repaid [1]. Therefore, the business can pay all the start-up costs and reduce the risk of getting into cash-flow problems [1].
13. Planning out all areas of the business helps to reduce the risk of failure. [1]

1. **Possible answer:** A supplier could impact the quality of the final products sold to consumers [1]. If the quality of the raw materials is poor, it will reduce the quality of the product [1], and this will damage the brand image of the business [1].
2. **Possible answer:** One way a pressure group could impact a business is that it could increase awareness among consumers of any unethical practices [1]. This could damage the business's brand image [1], which could reduce future sales [1].
3. **Any two from:** email; video calls; phone calls; social media [2]
4. **Possible answer:** If consumers do not want to purchase the products made by a business [1], then it may not receive enough revenue [1] so expensive advertising campaigns may need to be created to boost demand [1].
5. A [1]
6. B [1]
7. C [1]
8. **Possible answer:** Not all employees may be comfortable with digital communication and may need training to use it effectively on behalf of the business. [1] The training may cost money to deliver [1] and it will take time and reduce productivity while it is taking place [1].
9. **Possible answer:** One impact digital communication has on the marketing mix is promotion [1]. By using social media, a business can specifically target customers with advertisements that they are more likely to respond to [1]. This can lead to an increase in revenue for the business [1].
10. **Possible answer:** One way employment legislation might impact a business is that it could increase costs [1]. The business may need to invest time in implementing new rules [1] and, if it gets caught not abiding by them, it can be heavily fined [1].
11. $\dfrac{\$15\,000}{1.35}$ [1] = £11 111.11 [1]
12. £20 000 × 1.25 [1] = $25 000 [1]

1. **Possible answer:** A limitation of a public limited company is that there is a lack of control [1] if another shareholder wants to sell their shares to an investor [1]. This could impact the direction of the business when there may be a new shareholder with significant shares in the company [1].
2. **Possible answer:** An advantage of selling assets is that it can raise finance for the business without the need to lose ownership [1] or require repayments. This means the business could sell machinery that is no longer required [1] and therefore improve its cash-flow position [1].
3. **Possible answer:** If a new competitor enters the market, then a business may need to be more realistic on how much profit it expects to make [1]. If the new business is very competitive, this is likely to result in a decrease in sales to a business [1], which will reduce its profit [1].
4. **Possible answer:** Imports might increase owing to removal of tariffs by the UK government [1]. This makes importing cheaper [1], which encourages more of it [1].
5. **Possible answer:** If the strength of the pound weakens, it makes UK products cheaper [1]. Therefore, foreign customers may choose to purchase UK exports because they get better value for money [1]. This may result in an increase in sales [1].
6. **Possible answer:** Selling internationally may mean that the product has to be changed owing to different tastes in other countries [1]. Therefore, the business must conduct market research to identify how these consumer needs differ to its home market [1], which will increase costs [1].
7. A [1]
8. D [1]
9. **Any one from:** low prices; choice; high quality; convenience [1]
10. **Any one from:** EU; NAFTA; ASEAN [1]
11. This source of finance allows the business to gain a huge amount of capital without getting into debt [1], which means there are no repayments [1] and therefore are no changes to its fixed costs [1].

1. It allows the business to focus on products in the growth or maturity stage and not use up any resources on the declining product. [1]
2. **Any one from:** changing the product; changing the promotion; lowering the price; appealing to a new market segment [1]
3. **Possible answer:** The business could further develop the features of the product [1] to attract customers [1]. As a result, the improved product may better meet customer needs than others on the market [1].
4. **Possible answer:** If the business gets any negative backlash it could also damage the reputation of the partner sponsor (or vice-versa). [1]
5. The difference between sales price and the cost of production [1]
6. **Possible answer:** If the cost of producing the goods/services increases [1], the margin between cost of production and selling price will be smaller and the business may have to increase its prices [1]. This may result in customers looking to other brands and therefore a potential reduction in market share [1].
7. A [1]; B [1]
8. C [1]
9. **Possible answer:** Social media allows a business to collect instant feedback about its products [1]. Analysing the interactions, comments and shares of the promotion will help to gauge how customers feel [1]. The business can then make changes to the product based on the feedback [1].
10. B [1]
11. **Possible answer:** Having the correct balance between the 4Ps will enable the business to build an effective marketing strategy for its product [1] and this may attract more customers [1]. As a result, the business can gain a competitive advantage [1].

1. **Possible answer:** Workers may be less motivated due to the fact they are likely to work on the same tasks [1]. This may lead to differences in the quality of goods being produced [1], leading to more wastage and increased costs for the business [1].
2. **Any one from:** lower costs; increased productivity; improved quality; flexibility
3. Cost advantages gained by expanding the level of production [1]
4. a) 80 kilograms [1]
   b) 5 days [1]
5. A [1]
6. C [1]; D [1]
7. **Possible answer:** Responding to negative feedback shows customers that their opinion is valued [1]. This gives the business an opportunity to make improvements and offer unhappy customers a resolution [1]. It may also encourage affected customers to give the business another chance, helping it to retain its market share [1].

1. **Possible answer:** A business could increase net profit by reducing the cost of raw materials by finding a new supplier [1]. This would reduce the cost of sales [1], which in turn would increase net profit [1].
2. **Any two from:** raw materials; overtime wages; packaging; wages of temporary staff [2]
3. $\dfrac{£170\,000}{£360\,000}$ × 100 [1] = 47.22% [1]
4. Cost of sales = £550 000 – £150 000 = £400 000
   Net profit = £150 000 – £100 000 [1] = £50 000 [1]
5. a) $\dfrac{£30\,000}{£200\,000}$ × 100 [1] = 15% [1]
   b) £30 000 – £10 000 = £20 000
   $\dfrac{£20\,000}{£200\,000}$ × 100 [1] = 10% [1]
6. $\dfrac{£45\,000}{£400\,000}$ × 100 [1] = 11.25% [1]

7. **Possible answer**: Gross profit is calculated to show how much profit a business makes from selling goods or services after it has deducted the cost of sales (costs incurred directly) **[1]**. This means that if gross profit is low, the business is likely to review its variable costs **[1]** and consequently try to negotiate better deals **[1]**.

Pages 166–167 **Making Human Resource Decisions**

1. B **[1]**
2. A **[1]**
3. **Possible answer**: An application form helps the business to identify specific information about a candidate **[1]**, enabling it to assess which candidates have suitable skills and experience **[1]** and to select a smaller number of candidates to interview **[1]**.
4. **Possible answer**: A disadvantage of flexible working is that workers are not as closely supervised and can get easily distracted **[1]**. This may lead to a decrease in productivity **[1]**, which increases business costs **[1]**.
5. **Possible answer**: A benefit of part-time working to a business is that it can reduce staffing costs **[1]**. If the business only requires a limited number of hours to be worked every week **[1]**, then it does not have to pay full-time hours **[1]**.
6. **Possible answer**: A limitation of job enlargement is that the employee may not find this method motivating **[1]** if they are completing more complex tasks without being remunerated for it **[1]**. As a result, this could lead to an increase in labour turnover **[1]**.
7. **Possible answer**: A benefit of external recruitment to a business is that the new candidate could bring in new skills **[1]** that the business may not currently have available **[1]**. These new skills could help to make the business become more productive **[1]**.
8. **Any one from**: formal training; informal training; self-learning; observations **[1]**
9. **Possible answer**: A purpose of induction training is that it allows new members of staff to be made aware of the expectations of the business and the nature of their roles prior to starting **[1]**, which is likely to make it easier for them to integrate into the role **[1]** and ultimately increase business productivity **[1]**.
10. **Possible answer**: A limitation of training is that the employee may soon decide to look for a higher paid job elsewhere **[1]** because they have developed their skills from the training **[1]**. This means the money the business invested in the employee was lost **[1]**.
11. **Possible answer**: A business may choose to conduct performance reviews to hold their employees to account and set them clear targets to work against **[1]**. If the employees have clear targets and get feedback, it may increase motivation to achieve these targets **[1]** and productivity is likely to increase **[1]**.
12. **Possible answer**: Excessive communication may mean that the communication process takes longer **[1]** . This is because an employee may have to look over many emails **[1]** and may therefore be unable to quickly respond to something that might be urgent **[1]**.

Pages 169–186 **Practice Exam Paper 1: Investigating small business**

Section A

Question number	Answer / Indicative content	Mark
1 (a)	The only correct answer is C – Procurement	(1) AO1a
1 (b)	The only correct answer is C – Surveys	(1) AO1a
1 (c)	Award 1 mark for identification of a reason, plus 2 further marks for explaining this reason up to a total of 3 marks.	(3) AO1a=1 AO1b=2
	Access to cash is important because it is used to pay for supplies **[1]**. This means that the business is able to complete jobs booked in because it has the correct raw materials **[1]** and can maintain a reputation for completion of work.	
	If a business does not have enough cash, it will not be able to pay its bills **[1]**. This might mean that it becomes insolvent **[1]** and will therefore lead to business failure **[1]**.	
	Accept any other appropriate response. Answers that list more than one reason with no explanation will be awarded a maximum of 1 mark.	
1 (d)	Award 1 mark for identification of a drawback, plus 2 further marks for explaining this drawback up to a total of 3 marks.	(3) AO1a=1 AO1b=2
	Customers are unable to interact with the product **[1]**, which means that they cannot try it before they buy **[1]** and may lead to a high returns rate **[1]**.	
	Customers' account data can be vulnerable to cyber attacks **[1]**, which means that websites and apps need sophisticated encryption to protect them from malicious activity **[1]**, leading to high data management costs **[1]**.	
	Accept any other appropriate response. Answers that list more than one drawback with no explanation will be awarded a maximum of 1 mark.	
2 (a)	The only correct answers are A – Overdraft and D – Trade credit	(2) AO1a
2 (b)	The only correct answers are A – Survival and B – Market share	(2) AO1a
2 (c)	(i) 26 800 Cash outflows + Net cash-flow 18 200 + 8 600 (ii) 16 100 Net cash-flow + opening balance 7 500 + 8 600	Award full marks for correct numerical answer without working.	(2) AO2
2 (d)	Award 1 mark for identification of a disadvantage, plus 2 further marks for explaining this disadvantage up to a total of 3 marks.	(3) AO1a=1 AO1b=2
	Costs are increased **[1]** because businesses need to invest in protective equipment to ensure the safety of staff and customers **[1]**, which reduces their overall profit **[1]**.	
	Practices may need to be changed to comply with new laws **[1]**, which means that staff may need to go on training courses **[1]** and this leads to an increase in costs **[1]**.	
	Accept any other appropriate response. Answers that list more than one disadvantage with no explanation will be awarded a maximum of 1 mark.	
2 (e)	Award 1 mark for identification of an advantage, plus 2 further marks for explaining this advantage up to a total of 3 marks.	(3) AO1a=1 AO1b=2
	The owner is their own boss **[1]**, which means all decisions are made without having to consult anyone else **[1]**. Therefore the business can be run in the way that they see fit **[1]**.	

	There is only one owner [1], which means that any profits that the business makes are theirs to keep [1] and this is highly motivating.	
	Accept any other appropriate response. Answers that list more than one advantage with no explanation will be awarded a maximum of 1 mark.	
3 (a)	The only correct answer is B – Make a profit	(1) AO1a
3 (b)	Substitution into correct formula: Profit = Total revenue – Total costs April = 30 000 – 20 000 = **10 000** May = 60 000 – 40 000 = **20 000** June = 90 000 – 60 000 = **30 000** 10 000 + 20 000 + 30 000 Total profit = £60 000	Award full marks for correct numerical answer without working. / (2) AO2
3 (c)	Award 1 mark for identification of an advantage, plus 2 further marks for explaining this advantage up to a total of 3 marks. Trade credit operates on a 'get now, pay later' basis [1], which means businesses can procure materials without paying for them in cash [1] and this helps support cash-flow between jobs [1]. Trade credit can be a cheaper form of borrowing [1] as the supplier may not charge interest [1], which means the business doesn't have an increase in costs when taking suppliers before payment [1]. Accept any other appropriate response. Answers that list more than one advantage with no explanation will be awarded a maximum of 1 mark.	(3) AO1a=1 AO1b=2
3 (d)	Award 1 mark for identification of a disadvantage, plus 2 further marks for explaining this disadvantage up to a total of 3 marks. Participants may not express their honest and personal opinions [1] because they may be reluctant to say what they think, especially when their thoughts disagree with the views of another participant [1]. As a result, data collected many not be meaningful [1]. Data can be difficult to analyse [1] because participants are expressing judgements and opinions [1], which means additional research like questionnaires need to be conducted too [1]. Accept any other appropriate response. Answers that list more than one disadvantage with no explanation will be awarded a maximum of 1 mark.	(3) AO1a=1 AO1b=2
3 (e)	The number of skilled workers seeking employment would be relatively high (AO1b). This means that the business, when recruiting, may have applications from many highly experienced and/or capable workers, which gives it a competitive advantage on account of such a productive and efficient workforce (AO3a). Consumer income levels will fall (AO1b), which means customers are likely to buy less in quantity and choose cheaper items. This means businesses may need to lower their prices in order to compete (AO3a).	(6) AO1b=3 AO3a=3

Level	Mark	Descriptor
	0	No rewardable material.
1	1–2	• Demonstrates elements of knowledge and understanding of business concepts and issues, with limited business terminology used (AO1b). • Attempts to deconstruct business information and/or issues, finding limited connections between points (AO3a).
2	3–4	• Demonstrates mostly accurate knowledge and understanding of business concepts and issues, including appropriate use of business terminology in places (AO1b). • Deconstructs business information and/or issues, finding interconnected points with chains of reasoning, although there may be some logical inconsistencies (AO3a).
3	5–6	• Demonstrates accurate knowledge and understanding of business concepts and issues throughout, including appropriate use of business terminology (AO1b). • Deconstructs business information and/or issues, finding detailed interconnected points with logical chains of reasoning (AO3a).

Section B

Question number	Answer / Indicative content	Mark
4 (a)	Award up to 2 marks for linked points outlining a suitable aim. Award a maximum of 1 mark if points are not linked and/or if the answer is not contextualised. Social objectives [1]. Choosing local suppliers for its ingredients (AO2), therefore reducing its environmental impact. May have already established an industry-agreed price point [1]. Customer satisfaction [1]. Small touches like 'outstanding service' delivered by Adam's team (AO2) mean that customers want to come back time and again [1].	(2) AO2
4 (b)	The food (AO2) that The Hare on the Hill sells must meet customer needs and expectations. This means that the menu (AO2) must have a range of dishes (AO2) that cater for different types of customers who enjoy different flavours and have different dietary requirements (AO2) so that they enjoy their dining experience and are likely to recommend or return (AO3a). The quality of the food (AO2) must be fresh and seasonal (AO2) because it is promoting this information on its website. If the customer does not believe this to be the case, they could leave a bad review, which could damage the restaurant's (AO2) reputation (AO3a).	(6) AO2=3 AO3a=3

Level	Mark	Descriptor
	0	No rewardable material.
1	1–2	• Limited application of knowledge and understanding of business concepts and issues to the business context (AO2). • Attempts to deconstruct business information and/or issues, finding limited connections between points (AO3a).

Level	Mark	Descriptor
2	3–4	• Sound application of knowledge and understanding of business concepts and issues to the business context although there may be some inconsistencies (AO2). • Deconstructs business information and/or issues, finding interconnected points with chains of reasoning, although there may be some logical inconsistencies (AO3a).
3	5–6	• Detailed application of knowledge and understanding of business concepts and issues to the business context throughout (AO2). • Deconstructs business information and/or issues, finding detailed interconnected points with logical chains of reasoning (AO3a).

Question number	Answer / Indicative content		Mark
5 (a)	Substitution into correct formula: Quantity sold = Total revenue ÷ Selling price £7 980 ÷ £21.00 [1] 380 [1]	Award full marks for correct numerical answer without working.	(2) AO2
5 (b)	Substitution into correct formula: Profit = Total revenue − Total costs 7 980 − ((12.50 × 380) + 2 730) 7 980 − 7 480 [1] £500 [1]	Award full marks for correct numerical answer without working.	(1) AO2
5 (c)	Working in the food industry (AO2), the restaurant (AO2) must ensure that its food preparation area (AO2) is clean and complies with health and safety legislation. It has a responsibility to ensure that customers (AO2) don't become ill as this would damage its reputation and could lead to financial consequences or forceable closure (AO3a). The managers have a responsibility to keep staff safe in their working kitchen and restaurant area (AO2), which means that they have to ensure there is adequate signage to indicate where potential hazards are. This is to make sure that the chefs (AO2) and serving staff (AO2) don't injure themselves in the workplace (AO3a).		(6) AO2=3 AO3a=3

Level	Mark	Descriptor
	0	No rewardable material.
1	1–2	• Limited application of knowledge and understanding of business concepts and issues to the business context (AO2). • Attempts to deconstruct business information and/or issues, finding limited connections between points (AO3a).
2	3–4	• Sound application of knowledge and understanding of business concepts and issues to the business context, although there may be some inconsistencies (AO2). • Deconstructs business information and/or issues, finding interconnected points with chains of reasoning, although there may be some logical inconsistencies (AO3a).

Level	Mark	Descriptor
3	5–6	• Detailed application of knowledge and understanding of business concepts and issues to the business context throughout (AO2). • Deconstructs business information and/or issues, finding detailed interconnected points with logical chains of reasoning (AO3a).

Question number	Answer / Indicative content	Mark
6 (a)	Award 1 mark for stating one fixed cost The Hare on the Hill may have to pay. Rent or mortgage on the restaurant [1] Marketing of the menu [1] Chef's salary [1] Accept any other appropriate response. Do not accept fixed costs that would not be appropriate. Award 0 should the answer be incorrect or lacking in context.	(1) AO2
6 (b)	Award up to 2 marks for linked points outlining a suitable method of primary market research. Award a maximum of 1 mark if points are not linked and/or if the answer is not contextualised. Questionnaire [1] used to ask customers which cuisine they enjoy eating (AO2). This will help the business to understand what flavours to incorporate in future dishes [1]. Social media poll [1] asking customers to vote on pictures of puddings (AO2) that the business is planning to include in its next menu [1] so they know which will be most popular. Accept any other appropriate response. Do not accept methods that would not be appropriate. Award 0 should the answer be incorrect or lacking in context.	(2) AO2
6 (c)	• Targeted adverts ensure that the restaurant (AO2) is being advertised to likely and potential diners (AO2) based on their Internet history and digital footprint. This means that the money is being invested in reaching out to customers who are already interested in gastro dining (AO2) and who are therefore likely to engage with the promotion campaign, resulting in sales (AO3a). However, there is a financial cost attached to targeted adverts as the business has to purchase the information from data collection companies (AO3b). • Increasing the selling price of platters (AO2) increases the profit per unit, assuming there are no increases in the fixed or variable costs. This is because more revenue is being received for each sale (AO3a). However, some customers may not be prepared to pay the higher price for the food (AO2) and therefore levels of demand may fall, resulting in lower overall profit levels (AO3b).	(9) AO2=3 AO3a=3 AO3b=3

Level	Mark	Descriptor
	0	No rewardable material.
1	1–3	• Limited application of knowledge and understanding of business concepts and issues to the business context (AO2).

		• Attempts to deconstruct business information and/or issues, finding limited connections between points (AO3a). • Makes a judgement, providing a simple justification based on limited evaluation of business information and issues relevant to the choice made (AO3b).
2	4–6	• Sound application of knowledge and understanding of business concepts and issues to the business context, although there may be some inconsistencies (AO2). • Deconstructs business information and/or issues, finding interconnected points with chains of reasoning, although there may be some logical inconsistencies (AO3a). • Makes a judgement, providing a justification based on sound evaluation of business information and issues relevant to the choice made (AO3b).
3	7–9	• Detailed application of knowledge and understanding of business concepts and issues to the business context throughout (AO2). • Deconstructs business information and/or issues, finding detailed interconnected points with logical chains of reasoning (AO3a). • Makes a judgement, providing a clear justification based on a thorough evaluation of business information and issues relevant to the choice made (AO3b).

Section C

Question number	Answer / Indicative content	Mark
7 (a)	Award 1 mark for a correct market segment. Families with children who like outdoor activities [1] Care homes for therapeutic experiences [1] Schools for animal education days [1] Businesses promoting staff well being [1] Award 0 should the answer be incorrect or lacking in context.	(1) AO1a AO2
7 (b)	25.1 + 14.4 + 7.7 = 47.2%	(1) AO2
7 (c)	Award up to 2 marks for linked points outlining how the risk could be reduced. Award a maximum of 1 mark if points are not linked and/or if the answer is not contextualised. A business plan could be used to secure finance [1] for the purchase of more alpacas (AO2) as the document can be shared with banks and other investors who will look at it to see how capable Joanne (AO2) will be of paying back any money owed with interest [1]. A business plan would force Joanne (AO2) to consider all aspects of her business [1], which means she can determine if the idea of running an alpaca meet and greet business (AO2) is viable [1].	(2) AO2

	Accept any other appropriate response. Award 1 mark should the answer be undeveloped or lacking in context.	
7 (d)	• A loan is a large sum of money that can be repaid over a long period of time. This means Joanne (AO2) can spread the cost of borrowing into a number of smaller, more manageable, monthly payments, resulting in better management of cash-flow (AO3a). • The money is borrowed at a fixed rate of interest. This means that the alpaca experience business (AO2) is able to forecast its monthly repayments over a long period of time, even if interest rates increase. This means Joanne (AO2) is less affected should economic conditions change and customers have less money to spend on luxuries like outdoor animal experiences (AO3a). • However, loans do need to be paid back with interest and this repayment does increase fixed costs, which means that the cost of walking an alpaca may have to increase to cover the cost of the loan and to maintain profits (AO3b). • Retained profit is money that the alpaca business has in reserves generated from selling meet-and-greet experiences (AO2). • Using this money means that Joanne (AO2) does not need to go to a bank to borrow money to buy the animals (AO2), which means that she is not increasing her fixed costs (AO3). • However, retained profits can take years to generate and it is possible that Joanne (AO2) does not have access to the amount of money needed to buy the alpacas in savings and would therefore need to source external funds in order to achieve this expansion (AO3b).	(9) AO2=3 AO3a=3 AO3b=3

Level	Mark	Descriptor
	0	No rewardable material.
1	1–3	• Limited application of knowledge and understanding of business concepts and issues to the business context (AO2). • Attempts to deconstruct business information and/or issues, finding limited connections between points (AO3a). • Makes a judgement, providing a simple justification based on limited evaluation of business information and issues relevant to the choice made (AO3b).
2	4–6	• Sound application of knowledge and understanding of business concepts and issues to the business context, although there may be some inconsistencies (AO2). • Deconstructs business information and/or issues, finding interconnected points with chains of reasoning, although there may be some logical inconsistencies (AO3a). • Makes a judgement, providing a justification based on sound evaluation of business information and issues relevant to the choice made (AO3b).

| 3 | 7–9 | • Detailed application of knowledge and understanding of business concepts and issues to the business context throughout (AO2).
• Deconstructs business information and/or issues, finding detailed interconnected points with logical chains of reasoning (AO3a).
• Makes a judgement, providing a clear justification based on a thorough evaluation of business information and issues relevant to the choice made (AO3b). |

Question number	Answer / Indicative content	Mark
7 (e)	• Joanne (AO2) posts daily updates across all social media channels with highlights, photographs and promotions to engage her customers (AO1b). She uses her social media platforms to promote her availability for walks and meet-and-greets (AO2) and all her posts include a 'Buy Now' button, which can generate sales as customers can book activities (AO2) from her so very easily (AO1b / AO3a). • Customers are encouraged to comment on posts to identify different alpacas in the herd (AO2) or to post pictures of their walks with the different animals (AO2). This engages customers, reminds them of their happy day out with Joanne's animals and encourages other followers of the account to make their own arrangements for the outdoor experience (AO1b / AO2 / AO3a) so they too can share their own photographs. This means that Joanne is constantly providing customers with positive content and daily reminders about the time that they spent with their family and their friends (AO2), which makes them feel happy, thus reinforcing how satisfied they were with their day out, which will lead to customer recommendations and repeat purchase (AO1b / AO3a). • However, it is not just social media that generates customer enjoyment and satisfaction. Joanne needs to ensure that customers are well looked after whilst visiting the animals (AO2 / AO3b). This means ensuring that communication is effective so that customers understand what to wear on their visit (AO2), how to behave around the animals (AO2) and how to keep safe when walking the alpacas (AO2), which means that customers can enjoy themselves in an unfamiliar setting. (AO3b).	(12) AO1b=3 AO2=3 AO3a=3 AO3b=3

Level	Mark	Descriptor
	0	No rewardable material.
1	1–4	• Demonstrates elements of knowledge and understanding of business concepts and issues, with limited business terminology used (AO1b). • Limited application of knowledge and understanding of business concepts and issues to the business context (AO2). • Attempts to deconstruct business information and/or issues, finding limited connections between points (AO3a). • Draws a conclusion, supported by generic assertions from limited evaluation of business information and issues (AO3b).

| 2 | 5–8 | • Demonstrates mostly accurate knowledge and understanding of business concepts and issues, including appropriate use of business terminology in places (AO1b).
• Sound application of knowledge and understanding of business concepts and issues to the business context, although there may be some inconsistencies (AO2).
• Deconstructs business information and/or issues, finding interconnected points with chains of reasoning, although there may be some logical inconsistencies (AO3a).
• Draws a conclusion based on sound evaluation of business information and issues (AO3b). |
| 3 | 9–12 | • Demonstrates accurate knowledge and understanding of business concepts and issues throughout, including appropriate use of business terminology (AO1b).
• Detailed application of knowledge and understanding of business concepts and issues to the business context throughout (AO2).
• Deconstructs business information and/or issues, finding detailed interconnected points with logical chains of reasoning (AO3a).
• Draws a valid and well-reasoned conclusion based on a thorough evaluation of business information and issues (AO3b). |

Pages 187–204 **Practice Exam Paper 2: Building a business**

Section A

Question number	Answer / Indicative content	Mark
1 (a)	The only correct answer is B – Merger	(1) AO1a
1 (b)	The only correct answer is C – Tariff	(1) AO1a
1 (c)	Award 1 mark for identification of a benefit, plus 2 further marks for explaining this benefit up to a total of 3 marks. Buffer stock will be available [1], which means an increase in unexpected sales can still be catered for [1]. This means customers aren't turned away dissatisfied [1]. Buffer stock will be available [1], which means a delay in delivery will not cease trading [1]. This means customers aren't turned away dissatisfied [1]. Accept any other appropriate response. Answers that list more than one benefit with no explanation will be awarded a maximum of 1 mark.	(3) AO1a=1 AO1b=2

1 (d)	Award 1 mark for identification of a drawback, plus 2 further marks for explaining this drawback up to a total of 3 marks.		(3) AO1a=1 AO1b=2
	Employees will be off work whilst undertaking the training [1], which means that the business may need to employ temporary staff [1]. This leads to an increase in costs [1].		
	Externally-provided training usually incurs significant expense [1], which means that the business's costs will increase [1] and this reduces the overall profit [1].		
	Accept any other appropriate response. Answers that list more than one drawback with no explanation will be awarded a maximum of 1 mark.		
2 (a)	The only correct answers are A – Remuneration and D – Commission		(2) AO1a
2 (b)	The only correct answers are D – Speed and efficiency and E – Product knowledge		(2) AO1a
2 (c)	Substitution into correct formula: (£300 000 ÷ £600 000) × 100 [1] Answer: 50% [1]	Award full marks for correct numerical answer without working.	(2) AO2
2 (d)	Award 1 mark for identification of an advantage, plus 2 further marks for explaining this advantage up to a total of 3 marks.		(3) AO1a=1 AO1b=2
	Decisions are made at a local level [1], which means branches can alter their marketing mix to meet the needs of their customers [1] and therefore meet specific customer needs [1].		
	Increased autonomy [1], which increases the motivation of branch managers [1] and leads to increased staff retention [1].		
	Accept any other appropriate response. Answers that list more than one advantage with no explanation will be awarded a maximum of 1 mark.		
2 (e)	Award 1 mark for identification of an advantage, plus 2 further marks for explaining this advantage up to a total of 3 marks.		(3) AO1a=1 AO1b=2
	Production processes are automated [1], which means that the rate of manufacture can be increased [1] and this leads to increased levels of output [1].		
	As products are standardised [1], economics of scale can be achieved with raw materials bought in bulk [1], leading to lower variable costs [1].		
	Accept any other appropriate response. Answers that list more than one advantage with no explanation will be awarded a maximum of 1 mark.		
3 (a)	The only correct answer is A – Selling assets		(1) AO1a

3 (b)	Substitution into correct formula: (£10 000 ÷ £50 000) × 100 [1] Answer: 20% [1]	Award full marks for correct numerical answer without working.	(2) AO2
3 (c)	Award 1 mark for identification of an advantage, plus 2 further marks for explaining this advantage up to a total of 3 marks.		(3) AO1a=1 AO1b=2
	GPM measures how effectively a business converts revenue into profit [1] and, as this is measured as a percentage, comparisons can be made between businesses or between years of operation [1]. This allows businesses to evaluate their performance regardless of size [1].		
	GPM allows a business to review how efficiently it is using its resources as a percentage year-on-year [1], which can then help it to decide where cost cutting measures or changes to selling prices can be made [1]. This allows the business to remain competitive [1].		
	Accept any other appropriate response. Answers that list more than one advantage with no explanation will be awarded a maximum of 1 mark.		
3 (d)	Award 1 mark for identification of one way the market mix can influence competitive advantage, plus 2 further marks for explaining this up to a total of 3 marks.		(3) AO1a=1 AO1b=2
	An innovative product portfolio alongside an effective promotion campaign allows a business to differentiate its goods and services from others in the same marketplace [1]. This exceeds customer needs [1] and gives customers a reason to buy from the business instead of its competitors [1].		
	An online platform allows businesses to sell their products at a cheaper price [1] because they don't have the same overheads as those operating in a physical premises [1]. This means they are more attractive to price-sensitive shoppers [1].		
	Accept any other appropriate response. Answers that list more than one way with no explanation will be awarded a maximum of 1 mark.		

Question number	Indicative content	Mark
3 (e)	Product differentiation can enable a business to fill a gap in an existing marketplace (AO1b). This is because it has changed its product in such a way that meets the needs of an otherwise neglected customer base. This gives the business a competitive advantage. (AO3a)	(6) AO1b=3 AO3a=3
	Product differentiation, such as attaching a brand, can increase the perceived worth of a product (AO1b) and means customers will be prepared to pay a high price point. This increases the profit margin per sale. (AO3a)	

Level	Mark	Descriptor
	0	No rewardable material.
1	1–2	• Demonstrates elements of knowledge and understanding of business concepts and issues, with limited business terminology used (AO1b). • Attempts to deconstruct business information and/or issues, finding limited connections between points (AO3a).
2	3–4	• Demonstrates mostly accurate knowledge and understanding of business concepts and issues, including appropriate use of business terminology in places (AO1b). • Deconstructs business information and/or issues, finding interconnected points with chains of reasoning, although there may be some logical inconsistencies (AO3a).
3	5–6	• Demonstrates accurate knowledge and understanding of business concepts and issues throughout, including appropriate use of business terminology (AO1b). • Deconstructs business information and/or issues, finding detailed interconnected points with logical chains of reasoning (AO3a).

Section B

Question number	Answer / Indicative content	Mark
4 (a)	Award up to 2 marks for linked points outlining a suitable influence. Award a maximum of 1 mark if points are not linked and/or if the answer is not contextualised. Competitors [1] in the marketplace selling other models of dirt bikes (AO2) may have already established an industry agreed price point [1]. The target market [1]. Talaria is a premium product and customers are willing to pay a premium price [1] for their e-bikes (AO2).	(2) AO2
4 (b)	The function of the dirt bike (AO2) is important as if the *Sting R* (AO2) does not function in the way that is claimed, consumers will be dissatisfied and may as a result turn away from buying future e-bikes (AO2). This means lost repeat purchases (AO3a). Exceptional function such as nominal power of 8 kW (AO2) and fast acceleration (AO2) give the machine (AO2) a unique selling point. This means that bike dealers (AO2) are able to charge a premium price as customers see added value. (AO3a)	(6) AO2=3 AO3a=3

Level	Mark	Descriptor
	0	No rewardable material.
1	1–2	• Limited application of knowledge and understanding of business concepts and issues to the business context (AO2). • Attempts to deconstruct business information and/or issues, finding limited connections between points (AO3a).
2	3–4	• Sound application of knowledge and understanding of business concepts and issues to the business context, although there may be some inconsistencies (AO2). • Deconstructs business information and/or issues, finding interconnected points with chains of reasoning, although there may be some logical inconsistencies (AO3a).

Level	Mark	Descriptor
3	5–6	• Detailed application of knowledge and understanding of business concepts and issues to the business context throughout (AO2). • Deconstructs business information and/or issues, finding detailed interconnected points with logical chains of reasoning (AO3a).

Question number	Answer / Indicative content		Mark
5 (a)	Substitution into correct formula: (($5\,395 – $4\,595) ÷ $4\,595) × 100 [1] Answer: 17.41% [1]	Award full marks for correct numerical answer without working. Award 1 mark where candidate has answered to only 1 d.p.	(2) AO2
5 (b)	Substitution into correct formula: ($4\,595 + $5\,395) ÷ 2 [1] Answer: $4995 [1]	Award full marks for correct numerical answer without working.	(1) AO2
5 (c)	Talaria has a reputation for being a market leader in its field and is constantly looking for new ways to enhance its e-bikes (AO2). Undertaking extensive research and development means that it can maximise the function of its dirt bikes (AO2) and therefore promote unique selling points such as increased acceleration (AO2). This added value means customers are likely to purchase the *Sting R* over other competitors like Honda (AO2). Customers in this industry are looking for exhilaration and experience (AO2). By investing in the development of speed potential (AO2), the *Sting R* is attractive to adrenaline seekers (AO2). As technology develops, the design and function of the e-bike continues to evolve to ensure customers have the latest capabilities and are able to outperform their challengers in trial competitions and recreational fun (AO2).		(6) AO2=3 AO3a=3

Level	Mark	Descriptor
	0	No rewardable material.
1	1–2	• Limited application of knowledge and understanding of business concepts and issues to the business context (AO2). • Attempts to deconstruct business information and/or issues, finding limited connections between points (AO3a).
2	3–4	• Sound application of knowledge and understanding of business concepts and issues to the business context, although there may be some inconsistencies (AO2). • Deconstructs business information and/or issues, finding interconnected points with chains of reasoning, although there may be some logical inconsistencies (AO3a).

Question number	Answer / Indicative content	Mark
3	5–6	• Detailed application of knowledge and understanding of business concepts and issues to the business context throughout (AO2). • Deconstructs business information and/or issues, finding detailed interconnected points with logical chains of reasoning (AO3a).	

Question number	Answer / Indicative content	Mark
6 (a)	Award 1 mark for stating one method of distribution Talaria may use. Shop **[1]** to sell the dirt bikes (AO2) Retail space **[1]** to sell the dirt bikes (AO2) Website **[1]** to sell the dirt bikes (AO2) App **[1]** to sell the dirt bikes (AO2) Accept any other appropriate response. Do not accept methods that would not be appropriate. Award 0 should the answer be incorrect or lacking in context.	(1) AO2
6 (b)	Award up to 2 marks for linked points outlining a suitable impact. Award a maximum of 1 mark if points are not linked and/or if the answer is not contextualised. Loan capital **[1]** used to develop the latest e-bike (AO2) by applying to a bank will increase costs, as this will have to be repaid **[1]**. Share capital **[1]** used to develop the latest *Sting R* model (AO2) could dilute the ownership of the business **[1]**. Accept any other appropriate response. Do not accept impacts that would not be appropriate. Award 0 should the answer be incorrect or lacking in context.	(2) AO2
6 (c)	• Sponsorship promotes a positive brand. This is because the positive image and identity of riders like Bruce and Malachy Tetley (AO2) benefits the e-bike company (AO2) and lends it credibility. • Customers will perceive the dirt bike to be superior over other brands because the champion rider is promoting the brand. As a result, customers will be willing to pay a premium price for the product (AO3a). • Sponsorship can, however, damage the popularity of the e-bike (AO2) if the sponsored rider (AO2) does not perform well in competition. Poor performance (AO2) could harm how customers view the product and damage the reputation of the bike (AO2) as being a top performer in its field (AO3b). • Viral advertising means that thousands of potential customers will be made aware of the e-bike (AO2). • Increased awareness when customers are thinking about purchasing a dirt bike (AO2) means that they will be familiar with the *Sting R* (AO2) model and may choose that over a competitor's (AO2) equivalent simply because it is familiar to them (AO3a). • However, viral advertising can irritate customers if images and videos (AO2) flood their social media channels, causing customers to be put off or fatigued of the dirt bike (AO2) brand (AO3b).	(9) AO2=3 AO3a=3 AO3b=3

Level	Mark	Descriptor
	0	No rewardable material.
1	1–3	• Limited application of knowledge and understanding of business concepts and issues to the business context (AO2). • Attempts to deconstruct business information and/or issues, finding limited connections between points (AO3a). • Makes a judgement, providing a simple justification based on limited evaluation of business information and issues relevant to the choice made (AO3b).
2	4–6	• Sound application of knowledge and understanding of business concepts and issues to the business context, although there may be some inconsistencies (AO2). • Deconstructs business information and/or issues, finding interconnected points with chains of reasoning, although there may be some logical inconsistencies (AO3a). • Makes a judgement, providing a justification based on sound evaluation of business information and issues relevant to the choice made (AO3b).
3	7–9	• Detailed application of knowledge and understanding of business concepts and issues to the business context throughout (AO2). • Deconstructs business information and/or issues, finding detailed interconnected points with logical chains of reasoning (AO3a). • Makes a judgement, providing a clear justification based on a thorough evaluation of business information and issues relevant to the choice made (AO3b).

Section C

Question number	Answer / Indicative content	Mark
7 (a)	Award 1 mark for a correct service. Wedding photographer **[1]** Bridal hair and makeup **[1]** Wedding venue **[1]** Wedding flowers **[1]** Accept any other appropriate response. Award 0 should the answer be incorrect or lacking in context.	(1) AO1a AO2
7 (b)	46% + 28% = 74%	(1) AO2
7 (c)	Award up to 2 marks for linked points outlining a suitable impact. Award a maximum of 1 mark if points are not linked and/or if the answer is not contextualised. Wedding planners (AO2) may have different work ethics, depending on the country that they are from **[1]**. This can impact on timelines when planning collaboratively **[1]**. Wedding planners (AO2) may work in different times zones, depending on the country that they are in **[1]**. This can make communication difficult **[1]**. Accept any other appropriate response.	(2) AO2

| 7 (d) | • Offering wedding planners (AO2) commission on the wedding packages that they sell will give them (AO2) the incentive to promote elaborate weddings with luxurious dinners, high-end wedding stationery (AO2) and photography packages (AO2). By offering the bridal package organisers (AO2) a percentage of the overall cost of the event (AO2), the planners (AO2) will be motivated to persuade the brides and grooms (AO2) to buy their top-end packages.

• However, should the economic climate be challenging, customers may not be able to afford expensive celebrations and this means that regardless of how capable or persuasive the wedding planner is, they still won't be able to sell expensive packages. This means their commission is significantly reduced and they may start to look for alternative types of employment (AO3b).

• Planning a wedding (AO2) requires planners to be very creative, as each individual bride or groom (AO2) has a unique idea of how they want their big day (AO2) to look. Giving planners autonomy to make all decisions will mean that they are able to deliver a very bespoke package for each of the couples (AO2) they work with. Having this independence and control over each event (AO2) means the wedding planners (AO2) feel valued and trusted. As this is highly motivating, they will put together extra-special packages that lead to high levels of customer satisfaction (AO3a).

• However, wedding planners (AO2) who are inexperienced may struggle with very limited guidance and if they are not able to come up with their own ideas. The reception (AO2) packages they put together may be quite basic, leading to a poor reputation for the business should brides and grooms (AO2) not be fully satisfied (AO3b). | (9)
AO2=3
AO3a=3
AO3b=3 |

Level	Mark	Descriptor
	0	No rewardable material.
1	1–3	• Limited application of knowledge and understanding of business concepts and issues to the business context (AO2). • Attempts to deconstruct business information and/or issues, finding limited connections between points (AO3a). • Makes a judgement, providing a simple justification based on limited evaluation of business information and issues relevant to the choice made (AO3b).
2	4–6	• Sound application of knowledge and understanding of business concepts and issues to the business context, although there may be some inconsistencies (AO2). • Deconstructs business information and/or issues, finding interconnected points with chains of reasoning, although there may be some logical inconsistencies (AO3a). • Makes a judgement, providing a justification based on sound evaluation of business information and issues relevant to the choice made (AO3b).
3	7–9	• Detailed application of knowledge and understanding of business concepts and issues to the business context throughout (AO2). • Deconstructs business information and/or issues, finding detailed interconnected points with logical chains of reasoning (AO3a). • Makes a judgement, providing a clear justification based on a thorough evaluation of business information and issues relevant to the choice made (AO3b).

Question number	Answer / Indicative content	Mark
7 (e)	• Excellent customer service in the wedding industry (AO2) creates high levels of customer satisfaction (AO1b). • Customers planning their celebration (AO2) want their wedding planner (AO2) to be fully immersed in delivering the best day. This is because some feel it is their right to be treated like a VIP for their special occasion (AO2). This means they want to feel that their day and their needs are the full priority and focus of the planner (AO2) (AO3a). • However, there are high costs associated with hiring excellent wedding planners (AO2) who are able to deliver high levels of customer service through experience, industry contacts and interpersonal skills. This means that, in turn, the excellent service comes with a high price point which some couples (AO2) might not be able to afford (AO3b). • Other factors, such as price, may be more important than excellent customer service (AO1b). • Some customers may be price sensitive and will be more interested in the wedding package (AO2) being affordable. As a result, they may accept that they have to do a lot of their own planning, such as creating their own stationery or doing their own makeup for their event (AO2), to avoid the high cost of the planner working exclusively on their wedding (AO2). • A drawback of doing this is that the customer does not benefit from the relationships that the wedding planner (AO2) has established by working with various suppliers, such as local florists or photographers (AO2). Despite paying for a very basic package with Dubrovnik Weddings, the customer may still actually end up with very little in the way of savings (AO3b).	(12) AO1b=3 AO2=3 AO3a=3 AO3b=3

Level	Mark	Descriptor
	0	No rewardable material.
1	1–4	• Demonstrates elements of knowledge and understanding of business concepts and issues, with limited business terminology used (AO1b). • Limited application of knowledge and understanding of business concepts and issues to the business context (AO2).

		• Attempts to deconstruct business information and/or issues, finding limited connections between points (AO3a). • Draws a conclusion, supported by generic assertions from limited evaluation of business information and issues (AO3b).
2	5–8	• Demonstrates mostly accurate knowledge and understanding of business concepts and issues, including appropriate use of business terminology in places (AO1b). • Sound application of knowledge and understanding of business concepts and issues to the business context, although there may be some inconsistencies (AO2). • Deconstructs business information and/or issues, finding interconnected points with chains of reasoning, although there may be some logical inconsistencies (AO3a). • Draws a conclusion based on sound evaluation of business information and issues (AO3b).

3	9–12	• Demonstrates accurate knowledge and understanding of business concepts and issues throughout, including appropriate use of business terminology (AO1b). • Detailed application of knowledge and understanding of business concepts and issues to the business context throughout (AO2). • Deconstructs business information and/or issues, finding detailed interconnected points with logical chains of reasoning (AO3a). • Draws a valid and well-reasoned conclusion based on a thorough evaluation of business information and issues (AO3b).

ACKNOWLEDGEMENTS

The authors and publisher are grateful to the copyright holders for permission to use quoted materials and images, in particular the featured businesses Talaria UK, The Hare on the Hill, Calderbrook Alpacas and Dubrovnik Weddings.

Page 6 (bottom): Dundee Photographics / Alamy Stock Photo
All other images are © Shutterstock.com

Every effort has been made to trace copyright holders and obtain their permission for the use of copyright material. The authors and publisher will gladly receive information enabling them to rectify any error or omission in subsequent editions. All facts are correct at time of going to press.

Published by Collins
An imprint of HarperCollinsPublishers Ltd
1 London Bridge Street
London SE1 9GF

HarperCollinsPublishers
Macken House, 39/40 Mayor Street Upper,
Dublin 1, D01 C9W8, Ireland

© HarperCollinsPublishers Limited 2024

ISBN 978-0-00-864645-5

First published 2024

10 9 8 7 6 5 4 3 2

British Library Cataloguing in Publication Data.

A CIP record of this book is available from the British Library.

Authors: Cate Calveley, Stephanie Campbell, Helen Kellaway and Tony Michaelides
Publisher: Sara Bennett
Commissioning editor: Richard Toms
Editorial: Richard Toms, Charlotte Christensen and Jill Laidlaw
Cover Design: Kevin Robbins and Sarah Duxbury
Inside Concept Design: Sarah Duxbury and Paul Oates
Text Design and Layout: Jouve India Private Limited
Production: Bethany Brohm
Printed in India by Multivista Global Pvt.Ltd.

MIX
Paper | Supporting responsible forestry
FSC™ C007454

This book contains FSC™ certified paper and other controlled sources to ensure responsible forest management.

For more information visit: www.harpercollins.co.uk/green